Foreword

After I wrote *13 Steps to Bloody Good Luck* in 2014, I was inundated by readers' emails, tweets, Facebook posts and letters telling me that the book had helped them navigate their lives and careers. But one particular email drew my attention more than the others. The sender was a student who wondered whether it was possible to provide '13 Step' solutions to most of life's challenges. It got me thinking.

A few days later I was chatting with my friend, Sunil Dalal. Sunil and I have known each other from our days at Cathedral & John Connon School and St. Xavier's College, Mumbai. I have observed the discipline and perseverance with which he has worked towards building his family's fortunes. I gently put forth the idea that he write a book outlining the 13 Steps to wealth creation.

'Why me?' asked Sunil. 'I am neither a banker nor a Chartered Accountant. I have never managed a mutual fund or a financial services company. I don't even have an MBA in Finance!'

'Those are precisely the reasons why you should write this book,' I said to him. 'Any fool can make something simple sound complicated. It takes talent to make something complex sound simple. That's what you can do!'

It took a little more cajoling before I could get Sunil's acquiescence and he agreed to do it only after I consented to co-author the book with him. I'm glad that I persisted. Sunil has spent decades managing and growing wealth without being part of the banking and finance ecosystem. This makes him neutral to financial products and investment options. Who better to offer impartial advice?

The motivational speaker, Zig Ziglar, once joked 'Money isn't the most important thing in life, but it's reasonably close to oxygen on the *gotta-have-it* scale.' Given the undeniable fact that it forms a central part of our lives, I am delighted to present *13 Steps to Bloody Good Wealth* to my readers because I believe that Sunil has succeeded in distilling a lifetime of learning into 13 simple steps that almost anyone can follow.

Ashwin Sanghi
Mumbai, 2016

13 STEPS TO BLOODY GOOD WEALTH

ASHWIN SANGHI
SUNIL DALAL

First published by westland ltd in 2016

Published by Westland Books, a division of Nasadiya Technologies
Private Limited in 2023

No. 269/2B, First Floor, 'Irai Arul', Vimalraj Street, Nethaji Nagar, Alapakkam
Main Road, Maduravoyal, Chennai 600095

Westland and the Westland logo are the trademarks of Nasadiya Technologies
Private Limited, or its affiliates.

Copyright © Ashwin Sanghi, 2016

Ashwin Sanghi asserts the moral right to be identified as the author of
this work.

ISBN: 9789395767811

10 9 8 7 6 5 4 3 2 1

The views and opinions expressed in this work are the author's own and the facts
are as reported by him, and the publisher is in no way liable for the same.

All rights reserved

Typeset in PrePSol Enterprises Pvt. Ltd.
Printed at Nutech Print Services-India

No part of this book may be reproduced, or stored in a retrieval system, or
transmitted in any form or by any means, electronic, mechanical, photocopying,
recording, or otherwise, without express written permission of the publisher.

13 STEPS TO BLOODY GOOD WEALTH

Ashwin Sanghi is counted among India's highest selling English authors. He has written several bestsellers (*The Rozabal Line, Chanakya's Chant, The Krishna Key, The Sialkot Saga, Keepers of the Kalachakra, The Vault of Vishnu,* and *The Magicians of Mazda* in his *Bharat Series*) and two *New York Times* bestselling crime thrillers with James Patterson, *Private India* (sold in the US as *City on Fire*) and *Private Delhi* (sold in the US as *Count to Ten*). Ashwin also mentors, co-writes and edits titles in this popular *13 Steps Series* on subjects as diverse as Luck, Wealth, Marks, Health and Parenting.

He is a regular contributor to the Op-Ed pages of the *Times of India*. Ashwin has been included by *Forbes India* in their Celebrity 100 and by the *New Indian Express* in their Culture Power List. He is a winner of the Crossword Popular Choice Award 2012, Atta Galatta Popular Choice Award 2018, WBR Iconic Achievers Award 2018, the Lit-O-Fest Literature Legend Award 2018, the Kalinga Popular Choice Award 2021 and the Deendayal Upadhyaya Recognition 2023. He was educated at Cathedral and John Connon School, Mumbai, and St Xavier's College, Mumbai. He holds a Master's from Yale University, USA, and a D. Litt. (Honoris Causa) from JECRC University, Rajasthan. Ashwin lives in Mumbai with his wife, Anushika, and his son, Raghuvir.

Website: www.sanghi.in
Facebook: www.facebook.com/AshwinSanghi
Twitter: www.twitter.com/AshwinSanghi
YouTube: www.youtube.com/AshwinSanghi
Instagram: instagram.com/ashwin.sanghi
LinkedIn: www.linkedin.com/in/ashwinsanghi

Sunil Dalal is a serial entrepreneur. He has built multiple global technology businesses since taking over and redirecting UniDEL, a family-owned industrial automation group with worldwide alliances. Sunil is a member of the Young Presidents Organisation and is keen on nurturing entrepreneurial talent. He holds a Bachelor's degree in Mechanical Engineering & Management of Technology from Vanderbilt University, USA.

2008 was a defining year for many families as they lost their hard earned money in a bubble not of their making, but propelled by irrational exuberance and excessive leverage in the capital markets. Sunil saw certain investments collapse to as much as fifty per cent of their original value; some to even zero per cent. He knew then that he had to do something. Luck presented itself when his group couldn't find the appropriate technology to automate their private investment management through their family office. And that's when they were galvanised into action. They corralled all the know-how across their family office and technology businesses to build Asset Vantage (www.assetvantage.com), a unique software platform for wealth owners. Along the way they discovered that their solution was also a great fit for accounting firms, wealth advisors and institutions that want to harness the power of the platform to achieve optimal customer participation in developing customised financial strategies and plans.

You can connect with Sunil via the following channels:

Website: www.unidel-group.com/management/
Facebook: www.facebook.com/sunilkishoredalal/
Twitter: twitter.com/sunil_k_dalal
LinkedIn: www.linkedin.com/in/sunilkdalal

Introduction

What gives me the right to write a book about wealth? I'm not a banker, I don't have an MBA, nor have I ever worked in the financial services industry. But I indeed have been on the other side of the door as a consumer.

All of us have seen those lofty bank advertisements that make us feel as if the banks are right by our side, helping us through every phase of our lives. The reality could not be further away from the truth. The simple truth is that all those banks have great ad agencies.

I am reminded of my nightmarish dealings with some of these banks, which are household names, when they were apparently helping me manage my money. What they actually did was pull a fast one on me. One bank skimmed 1% off a foreign exchange transaction when it should have been 0.05%. Another made me run from pillar to post to three branches to get a simple direct debit cell phone connection completed. A third lost 25% of my equity portfolio due to a badly-conceived investment strategy.

The American cartoonist, Kin Hubbard, is believed to have once commented that the safe way to double one's money is simply to fold it over once and put it inside your pocket! Possibly Hubbard had dealt with financial institutions!

I'm narrating these incidents because I'm sure you have been at the receiving end of such situations too. Whether it is being sold the wrong product, charged extra fees, or not having your queries answered, all of us have suffered at the hands of these faceless bureaucracies. It boils down to a massive industry structural problem where the banks and their employees are often financially incentivised in ways that are fundamentally not in the consumer's best interest.

These establishments often take advantage of our ignorance, sometimes knowingly and sometimes due to their sheer bureaucracy. During my troublesome interactions with them, I learned some real life lessons, which I feel need to be shared. If you can benefit from my experience, it will hopefully make your learning faster and easier.

Getting mistreated like this by such reputed, global entities fired up my desire to learn everything about how the wealth management industry works. Over the last ten years, this put me on the path of a fascinating journey. I read books, opinion pieces and reports. I learned from my colleagues and picked the minds of industry veterans for their wisdom.

I also learned in traditional classrooms of the executive education programmes at Wharton, Columbia University and the Indian School of Business. But the best learnings came from talking to people, navigating real-life situations and, frankly, by applying lots of common sense.

I have taken some of those experiences that I went through as a consumer to demystify the subject of wealth. It's this marriage of theory, my personal research, and practical experience over the last many years that has manifested itself into this book. Hopefully, this book will be your step-by-step guide to becoming a better personal money manager.

I believe that no industry can prosper over long periods of time unless vendors and consumers can grow and profit together. Unfortunately, the financial services industry is one of the last in the world that profits in ways that doesn't always benefit the customer. However, the practice is changing for the good as we speak. The power of technology is disrupting the current status quo to bring empowerment to the end consumer. So whether you are making an online payment transaction or investing in a financial product, you will be able to execute this in a simple, transparent, cost-effective and secure environment with the use of technology. In the spirit of full disclosure, I firmly stand in the camp of the end-consumer and hope my friends in the financial services camp will respect that.

I have some definitive views on wealth creation and growth. But I am happy to be challenged and will gladly change my stance when proven wrong. My DNA is about taking complex situations and simplifying them into practical, actionable solutions, propped upon the firm foundations of facts. I hope that this book delivers just that: simple solutions to seemingly complex matters.

The Irish playwright, Oscar Wilde, once said, 'When I was young I thought that money was the most important thing in life; now that I am old I know that it is.' So join me in this exploration of one of the most important things in life.

Sunil Dalal
Mumbai, 2016

Step 1

Define what wealth means to you

The Mahabharata has a curious side story. One day, the Kauravas attacked a village under King Virata's rule and stole all of their cattle. The Pandavas were forced to step in and save the king from losing his entire herd.

While it's just a minor detail, I have always wondered about this. The greatest warriors in Indian history used to steal cows? Arjuna has always been a likeable character. A dashing chap, righteous, and with a killer aim to boot. I mean, what's not to like? But to think of this hero stepping in to prevent cattle theft sounds a little odd.

But turn the pages of history and with each century the concept of wealth changes. Ten thousand years ago, wealth could have been a sharp spear or axe. Eight thousand years ago, it could have been a basket of fish that you exchanged for a bag of rice. Our Indian ancestors living many millennia ago bartered with cowrie shells that spread as far as China and Africa. In contrast, today we see cowrie shells on beach shacks, hippie motels and braided in the hair of Rastafarians. To our ancients, these people may have been unimaginably wealthy.

Similarly, in the age of the Mahabharata, cattle was a commodity. Could the ancients ever have imagined a time when humans would brandish rectangles of plastic that, with one swipe, could buy everything from grain to airplanes? They surely would never have imagined that there would come a time when money would be bits of data encrypted over large networks.

So let's always remember this: money is merely a concept, albeit the most powerful concept ever to grip human consciousness. It runs our world and turns our lives topsy-turvy. Many say that to master money is to master life itself!

There is an Urdu couplet that says: *Paisa khuda toh nahin par, khuda ki kasam, khuda se kam bhi nahin.* Money isn't God but, by God, it's no less than God either. There's also the proverb which says that money can't buy you happiness, but it can buy you the kind of misery you prefer!

Frankly, I like to think of the machinations of money as a lifelong game that adults like to play. It's a game in which earning more and more can become an obsession. But one needs to remember that when one dies, everything that one has earned is left behind.

There is simply no way to carry it into the next life as the ancient Egyptians believed.

So what exactly is wealth?

Wealth is a shifty, dynamic thing. Just as the concept of what constitutes money has changed over years, the idea of what is wealth can be different from one person to the next even though they may live in the very same neighbourhood. It can also vary from time to time for the very same person. I remember when I was in college, a *vada-pav* and soft drink at the neighbourhood restaurant were a big treat for my friends and me. While I would still relish it, yet that particular treat no longer offers the same level of excitement.

Whether you're wealthy or not also depends on where you live and to whom you're comparing yourself. A person in America earning $50,000 per year is squarely amongst the median household earners. But compared to the rest of the world, he or she is in the top 1% of the wealthy. You can live like a king with a salary of 20,000 rupees per month in a village, but in Mumbai you are shunted to the margins of daily existence with that kind of money.

So tell me, what does being wealthy mean to you? I understand that to be able to define exactly what wealth means to us can be a bit of a bouncer. It is so tied up with each and every aspect of our lives that to think about its significance is to examine every nitty-gritty of our daily routines, aspirations and desires.

I can ease you along on this path. Here's a little structure to think about the essentials of wealth.

What do we need money for?

- **Basic needs:** First and foremost, all of us need money to cover the very basics. The holy trinity of *roti-kapda-makaan* or food, clothing and shelter constitutes the foundation of our everyday existence. The world runs on generating an income for these simplest of human necessities. The trinity are the non-negotiable part of your wealth.
- **Higher needs:** Now come aspirational needs, the 'nice-to-haves'. A second home, jewellery, investments. I like to place raising enough capital for one's (maybe yet unborn) children's education and marriage in this category as well.
- **Financial independence:** I take this one seriously. Each person is responsible for their own success and comfort. While liberalisation has opened the doors for unmitigated success, it has also taken away the hopes of unlimited government hand-outs or subsidies.
- **Retirement:** This one is important. In India, the concept of planning one's retirement

is only now taking root. If you're lucky, you could end up with a job that pays you a decent enough pension. But most people in the private sector do not have this luxury. Traditionally, people's children have been their retirement fund. But I don't believe in doing that. I want to be self-sufficient and comfortable after I retire, without having to worry about money and without needing assistance from my kids. How am I preparing to do that? By planning for it.

We'll soon get into the details of how to set and plan one's financial goals, but let's not get ahead of ourselves. Now that we have gone through the various reasons and requirements for wealth, ask yourself this question: 'Am I wealthy?'

Are you wealthy?

Here's a little nugget for you. In a survey conducted by UBS, Americans with assets of $1 million to $5 million were asked if they considered themselves wealthy. Only 28% of them said yes.

Please remember that these are some of the richest people in the world. Why do they not consider themselves wealthy? When questioned further, for some, being truly wealthy meant having enough cash to handle any expenses without liquidating their assets. For others, being wealthy just meant 'having peace of mind'.

I was reminded of a discussion at a lively party. I was surrounded by friends and family members of various ages, occupations and at different stages of life. We were enjoying ourselves with good conversation over *paneer pakodas* and chilled beer when the talk turned to money. At this point the host asked everyone what wealth meant to them.

Initially, the responses were a little stilted. But by the time that the biryani was served people really began to take the question in their stride. This led to some interesting discussions. Overall, a great evening and now I get to present to you some samples from my host's thoroughly unscientific poll:

- 'To me, wealth is my experience, knowledge, good health and family,' said Ashok, sixty-six years old.
- 'In terms of material wealth, I think you can say you're wealthy when you decide to be satisfied with what you have. But you should have earned it ethically and it should be beneficial to others, not just yourself,' said Rahul, age thirty-six.
- 'To me, wealth is a feeling of security but only when it comes with a combination of monetary assets along with knowledge, experience,

and contentment,' offered Anita, around thirty-five years old.

I remember one of my college teachers telling me that money could buy you a pretty good dog but not the wagging of its tail. The wide variety of dinner responses is beautifully summed up by the Pulitzer prize winning writer Carl Sandburg who said, 'Money is power, freedom, a cushion, the root of all evil...and the sum of blessings.'

Is wealth everything?

One of my friends flipped the question around and posed it to me. Here's what I told him. 'I want to be wealthy so that I may have the full freedom to pursue my life's ambitions, without being shackled down by monetary constraints.'

The American television host, Johnny Carson, had once said, 'The only thing that money gives you is the freedom of not having to worry about money.' That pretty much summed up my view.

Look, we discussed earlier why one needs money. But I also love my work. So once I have made sure my family is secure and comfortable, wealth for me is about what I can do with it to positively impact the rapidly changing face of the businesses I'm involved with and, in the process, change the lives of our customers and team members. In Roosevelt's words,

'Happiness is not in the mere possession of money. It lies in the joy of achievement, in the thrill of creative effort.'

Personally, I am hugely motivated by the idea of solving deep-rooted problems through technology. Some of these problems and opportunities include making a social impact, which is another objective that drives me.

There are times when this has required me to take financial risks. Things were not always comfortable. I have faced situations where I had no real support because the typical investors I pitched my plan to did not believe in my vision. I did not want to lose control to such investors, who might not have understood the problems we were trying to solve.

Being financially independent, freed me from such constraints and gave me the liberty to pursue the endeavours that I believed in without seeking outside assistance. And my belief has worked for me thus far. The comedian Groucho Marx quipped that money '... frees you from doing things you dislike. Since I dislike doing nearly everything, money is handy.'

This is not to say that one should not enjoy wealth. Of course you should. Take pleasure in travel, food and the occasional indulgence in gadgets or fashion. But you have to ask if your real happiness is tied to these material concepts? I can say with confidence that it is not.

Millionaires, wealth advisors, finance writers and gurus will fill your head with their expert opinions on what being wealthy means. I'm no wizard. I'm just a regular guy who happened to have certain ideas about wealth and how to create and grow it. In my life I have gone through many ups and downs. My family business went from boom to bust, and I pulled it back on its feet. I feel I have something worthwhile to share about how I managed to turn things around.

Key Takeaway

Think about what being wealthy means to you. The 'you' part is fundamental because no two persons will offer the same definition of wealth. Only once you know what being wealthy means to you will you really be in a position to work towards it.

Step 2

Make a plan

Is it a coincidence that in 12th century England, the word 'wealth' meant well-being and happiness? It seems that people in the so-called dark ages had a better idea of what wealth is (or what it should be). In the same spirit, American poet and philosopher, Henry Thoreau said, 'Wealth is the ability to fully experience life.'

To put it in perspective, let's go back to the party where people were confessing what wealth meant to them. By the time dessert was served, my friend modified his survey question and slyly asked his guests what they would do if they were to win *Kaun Banega Crorepati*. Now, there were many veterans at the party who looked unimpressed by the thought. They politely ignored the question and concentrated on their *jalebis*.

But it was the younger bunch, the people in their mid-twenties and early thirties, that had interesting responses. All of them spoke about pursuing their passions. Some said they would travel, some wished to train as chefs or scuba divers, yet others had ideas for apps that would apparently change the world.

But tell me, do you really need ten crore rupees to chase your dreams? I can assure you that if you're not travelling now, you will not travel when you have a crore, five crores or even ten crores. We often create mental obstacles for ourselves, blaming our life's situations for not going after our heart's true desires because we're afraid of failure. The French fashion designer, Coco Chanel, famously said, 'There are people who have money and then there are people who are rich.'

For me, it was never about becoming wealthy. I just wanted to do what I loved. Yes, it may sound clichéd but you know what? All clichés are based in some truth. A casual study of most billionaires around the world will show you that when they started out, their motive was not to become super rich but to do something great. And *that* is the secret of wealth.

What's your hustle?

Finding what you love is the most important part of the puzzle. Uncovering your goals in life is the biggest favour you will do yourself. When you find your passion, loving the hustle will not be a chore, but something that will govern your life.

Having a dream is a must. It keeps you going and lets you forget the challenges of the daily grind. It helps you face the curve balls life throws at you. And remember that a goal is simply a dream with one's eyes open.

So here's what I believe: wealth is about passion. Don't obsess about money, but do be mindful. Be patient, but also don't hesitate to grab the bull by its horns when the right opportunity presents itself. Ride the wave and find your greatness.

The Rockefeller Rule

'If your only goal is to become rich, you'll never achieve it,' said John Rockefeller, America's first billionaire. His point was simple: when the only thing you care about is making money, no amount of money is ever enough.

Adjusting for inflation, his fortune upon his death in 1937 stood at $336 billion, accounting for more than 1.5% of the American economy, making him the richest person in US history. His foundations pioneered the development of medical research and were instrumental in the eradication of hookworm and yellow fever. Rockefeller was also the founder of the University of Chicago. Today, multiple plazas, buildings, awards and foundations are named after him.

A little-known fact: a meeting with Swami Vivekananda inspired him to use his wealth to help the poor and needy. All of this is to say that wealth is multi-dimensional. How you earn it, how you spend it, and what you make of it are unique. Just like your personality.

Hitting the jackpot

It's tempting to think of wealth building as a fairy tale. But here's the truth: Unlike Cinderella's story, wealth does not arrive overnight. Most wealthy people (and you could be one of them) are years in the making. As you will see later, on average, an Indian billionaire has spent almost forty years getting there. And in order to spend that much time reaching a goal, you must have a plan.

But remember to be flexible. Think of your plan as an optimal GPS route taking you from one place to another. The route may require you to take a flyover when you leave home, but if an accident has clogged up the flyover, you may need to reroute through interior roads to reach your destination on time. Similarly, be firm in your convictions and keep the end in mind, but don't be blind and get stuck in traffic either.

When I got involved in my family business in 1991, we were on the brink of collapse without even knowing it. India's economic liberalisation was taking its toll on us. Our products and services were rapidly getting obsolete. So frankly, at that time my dream was simply for the business to survive. But the journey took me from boom to bust to another boom with many twists and turns. In fact, our story became the subject of a case study at the London Business School and is taught in the 'Entrepreneurship in the Emerging Markets' course.

After we became financially secure, my dream got redefined each year, moving from domestic leadership in our sector to aspiring to global dominance. The goal has kept me going through tough times like the financial crisis of 2008. It has allowed me to not only survive, but come out stronger. Reinvention will help you stay young, current and not gloat over your past successes.

Quantify your goals

In recent years, Narayan Murthy, the founder of Infosys, has popularised this quote by Deming, the quality guru, 'In God we trust, everybody else brings data to the table.'

This statement always makes me chuckle, but it's also been my personal mantra. As an engineer, I have no patience for *fundas* and theories that don't have a basis in fact. Numbers have always been my friends because numbers don't hide and numbers don't lie. So the first step towards realising your dream is to quantify your goals into solid, tangible numbers that you can work towards.

Then assess the current situation. Take stock, do a recce. In financial terms, calculate your net worth. Net worth is the value of everything you own (your assets), minus everything you owe (your liabilities). But it's one thing to find out what your net worth *is* and quite another to find out what it *should be*.

It can seem mind boggling to try to gauge how much your net worth should be but there's a simple formula to calculate the target at your age with your current income.

$$\frac{\text{Average}}{\text{Net Worth}} = \frac{\text{Age} \times \text{Pretax Annual Household Income}}{10}$$

Let's consider Ragini, a 41-year-old who makes Rs 10,00,000 per year. She has investments that return another Rs 1,00,000 every year. According to our formula, Ragini's net worth should be:

$$\frac{41 \times (10,00,000 + 1,00,000)}{10}$$

The result of the above formula is Rs 45.10 lakhs. This is what Ragini's net worth *should be* at her present age and income level. Please take this formula with a pinch of salt. It tends to work better for people who are over forty years old. No single formula like the one above is always accurate. Obviously, for each age and income bracket, there is a certain expected amount of wealth. Anything significantly higher than that would be considered wealthy.

If you're feeling overwhelmed by the formula above, hold on. Slow and steady always wins. Breaking up the goal into smaller chunks makes it easier and approachable. I'd suggest splitting your monetary goals into short, medium and long-term goals. That is the essence of good planning.

- **Short-term goals:** Achieve within one to two years: Examples could involve buying the latest gadgets, an iPhone or a DSLR camera. I would place taking an exotic vacation in this category too.
- **Medium-term goals:** Achieve within two to five years: These could include buying a new car or home. I would add preparing for any hitch in your plans under this too: a recession, a layoff, a bad investment. Being fully prepared for them should be high on your medium-term goals.
- **Long-term goals:** More than five years: Saving for your children's education or wedding, your retirement. Also, the most important, getting your average net worth up to the mark!

Dale Carnegie narrated a story of two men who were out chopping wood. One of them took no breaks and only stopped briefly for lunch. The other one took many breaks during the day and a short nap after lunch. When the day came to an end, the cutter who had taken no breaks was perturbed to see that his relaxed colleague had chopped more wood than he had. He said, 'I simply do not understand! Each time I looked you were sitting down for a break. Yet you end up chopping more wood than me!' The relaxed woodcutter asked, 'By any chance did you notice that whenever I was sitting down, I was also sharpening my axe?' This is why Steven Covey calls planning 'sharpening the axe.' Planning is the difference between being reactive and proactive.

Of course, the overall challenge in planning is that life goes on in parallel. Often, your primary job takes so much out of you that you are left with little time or inclination to plan. Let me end this chapter with a small story to explain the challenges involved in planning.

Planning while life goes on

A coronary surgeon took his vehicle to his dealer for a scheduled service. He took out some time for a friendly conversation with the garage owner who was also a competent mechanic. 'So tell me, doctor,' began the mechanic, 'I've been thinking about what we both do for a living.'

'Yes?' asked the surgeon.

'Well, just think about it,' said the mechanic. 'I check how the engine is running, I open it up, I repair the valves and then I put it all back together so that it works perfectly. You and I do pretty much the same job don't we? And yet you earn ten times of what I do. That doesn't seem very fair.'

The surgeon thought about the mechanic's comment for a moment and then gently replied, 'Try doing everything that you just said while the engine is running.'

Your attempt to plan for wealth is a little bit like that. You have to do it while life around you still goes on!

Key Takeaways

- Quantify your goals. Use the formula within this chapter to create a target net worth based on your age and income.
- Classify your goals into short-term, medium-term and long-term.

Step 3

Beat inflation

Last year, I went to my high school alumni meet. It was incredible. I saw some classmates after over two decades. We all hugged, back-slapped and took potshots at each other for our receding hairlines and expanding waistlines. For three glorious hours it felt as though we had turned into skinny seventeen-year-olds.

Again and again we said, 'Remember when...' and relived the good old days. As the evening wore on, we showed each other pictures of our kids and spouses, and laughed about the times we happily enjoyed ourselves on non-existent budgets. One pertinent topic of discussion was how cheap everything used to be back in the day, be it a bottle of Coke (or Thums Up which was the favourite of the eighties) at two rupees or a cone of *channa* for twenty-five paise.

It was similar to a discussion that I would often have with my grandfather. He would tell me that a plate of two samosas cost one anna in 1947. One-sixteenth of a rupee! Today, a single samosa would cost around ten rupees. In effect, the price of samosa has gone up 320 times in 69 years.

My father tells me that an apartment in South Bombay cost thirty-four rupees per square foot in 1961. Today those same apartments sell for around seventy-five thousand per square foot. In effect, the price per square foot went up 2205 times in 55 years.

Nostalgia tends to make people see 'the good old days' through rose-coloured lenses, but in this case there is a simple explanation for making the prices of things seem so low: inflation. Because prices have spiked so much since my friends and I saw each other, everything seems cheap in hindsight!

Inflation is like sin. Every government denounces it, and yet every government follows policies that lead to it. Inflation is a particularly modern Indian problem. It is eating away into the actual value of our money. It's no wonder then that it has felled governments, roused the generally apathetic *janata* and made activists out of regular middle-class blokes.

The economist, Milton Friedman, correctly remarked that 'inflation is taxation without legislation.' Legislation is required to recover tax from you but none is required to achieve exactly the same result via inflation.

Life is tough when the grocery store bill or the running metre at the petrol pump start giving you mini panic attacks. It makes daily life a chore. What's more, inflation also affects our future planning. You may be diligent, putting away money for a rainy day around the corner. But inflation is actually cutting your returns, and in some cases, even inducing negative growth. With a fixed income, you're able to afford less and less. In a high inflation country like India, then, it is absolutely crucial to beat inflation and stay ahead of it.

Inflation: The illusion of wealth

India's inflation rate has been on the rise over the last decade. At a compounded annual rate of nearly 8%, it's a major wealth-destroyer for people across classes and regions. The American stand-up comic, George Gobel, rightly observed, 'If inflation continues to soar, you're going to have to work like a dog just to live like one.'

Besides having a bearing on the daily price of commodities, inflation affects the interest rates paid on savings and mortgages. It also influences pensions and other government benefits. You might be saving your money diligently but the actual value of your hard-earned cash is constantly being diluted because of rising prices.

While we all crib and stew to let off some steam, inflation has serious economic consequences for our lives. So tell me, what exactly have you done about inflation?

Let's take the example of an MBA degree from an Indian Institute of Management (IIM). In 1999–2001, a two-year MBA at any of the IIMs used to cost about three lakh rupees. Fifteen years later the same degree costs twenty-five lakhs. What's interesting is that while the expenses for the degree have increased by over eight times, the average starting salary of an IIM graduate has gone from five lakh rupees per year in 2001 to about twenty lakhs per year today, an increase of only four times.

The implications are clear. If you're planning for your children's education, but don't have the discipline to set aside funds that not only add up in the next eighteen or so years, but also beat inflation, you should be worried.

Growth vs. Inflation

When you beat inflation, your wealth grows automatically, regardless of rising prices. This is when you gain true freedom.

You've been reading all these words for a while now. Let's go back to my pet peeve, yes, numbers. We have been talking about beating inflation. Now is the time to actually see how it affects our savings and investments.

Between 2004 and 2014, prices rose by about 8.4% per year, which means that inflation during these ten years was at 8.4%. We can look at this from another angle. Let's say in 2005, you were spending Rs 10,000 per month on living expenses. Because of inflation, in 2015 you need to spend Rs 22,500 per month to maintain the same lifestyle.

Against this inflation rate of 8.4%, let's compare the various investment scenarios from 2004 to 2014:
- The bond index gave a return of 7.8% per year. In effect, if you invested in bank fixed deposits in 2004, by 2014 your money would have actually reduced in value by 5.4% because of inflation.
- Certain bond funds managed to marginally outpace inflation, returning 9% per year. In effect, if you invested in bond funds, your money had no real growth.
- The BSE Sensex returned 15.7% per year and diversified equity mutual funds returned 20.9% per year. So, if you invested in equity in the same period, your money would have seen real growth of 7.3% per year and 12.5% per year respectively after adjusting for inflation.

To summarise, in the above example, equity is one of the few asset classes that beat inflation over extended periods of time. We will go into the details of various types of investment categories later but the point I'm making here is that only certain investment classes allow you to beat inflation and earn some real returns.

The Weimar Hyperinflation Crisis of 1923

After losing World War I, Germany was compelled to pay huge reparations to the victors. However, Germany was not allowed to use its own currency to meet these commitments. Germany started selling their currency at any price to get foreign currencies with which to pay the debt.

Adolf Hitler's rise to power was partly fuelled by crazy hyperinflation. Prices were doubling every 3.7 days and inflation was at a staggering 29,500%. A loaf of bread, which cost 250 marks in January 1923 was available for 200,000 million marks in November 1923! People were collecting their wages in suitcases. One person, who left his suitcase unattended, found that a thief had stolen the suitcase but not the money.

Some people, though, actually made money during the crisis. One man borrowed money to buy a herd of cattle and paid back his full loan by selling exactly one cow from the herd.

Real vs. Nominal Returns

Remember the joke about the man who called and ordered a large cheese pizza. The order clerk asked him whether he would like it cut into six or eight slices. 'Eight,' he replied, 'I'm really hungry today.' That explains the difference between real and nominal returns because nominal returns can often be an illusion.

The real rate of return is calculated by adjusting for price changes caused over time by inflation. The generation of real wealth depends on the bottom line. What's more, you may need to further deduct expenses, taxes and fees if your money is professionally managed.

Let's consider an investment that gives you a return of 10% per year. If you invested Rs 100 in 2004 it would become Rs 259.37 by 2014. But that's only the nominal return. What happens after tax and inflation are deducted?

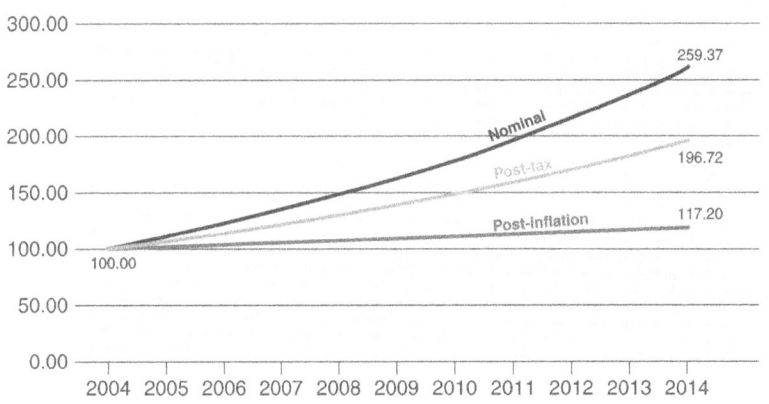

The graph above shows us the huge effect inflation has on long-term financial planning. Most of us look at the nominal return, not bothering to see that the curve dips when taxes are paid, and further dips when inflation is factored in.

The American baseball player, Sam Ewing, accurately observed that 'Inflation is when you pay fifteen dollars for the ten-dollar haircut you used to get for five dollars when you had hair.'

If this step has left you feeling worried about how to earn well, pay taxes, beat inflation and yet live comfortably, don't worry. That's why I wrote this book. Read on.

Key Takeaways

- Only certain investment classes (like equity) allow you to beat inflation.
- The effect of inflation and taxes means that real returns are far lower than nominal returns.

Step 4

Plan your expenses

To some people, getting rich is about spending less. To others, it's about earning more. Unfortunately if you're earning more and spending more, you'll just stay where you are. It's like running on a treadmill. Factor in inflation and, in the long run, your returns will be negative. The Greek philosopher, Epictetus, rightly observed that, 'Wealth consists not in having great possessions, but in having few wants.'

There are numerous high-income professionals who have ended up with no savings despite a successful career because they lived a high-consumption lifestyle without having an expense plan. Planning your current expenses is a part of investing in your future. When you take time out and make an expense plan, you're doing your future self a favour and trust me, you will thank your past self for this. One needs to make a mental note of what the famous painter Pablo Picasso said. 'I'd like to live as a poor man with lots of money.'

You must gain control over your money or the lack of it will forever control you. It sounds old-fashioned, but honestly, being thrifty never went out of style. Frugality has been an important part of a many a billionaire's success. On the flipside, the world of the rich and famous is also littered with many illustrious business families that have fallen upon hard times. This happened because they failed to instil the value of money in their children.

When these heirs and heiresses grew up and came into money, they had no clue about the virtues of frugality, of growing money as opposed to blindly spending it. Many of these erstwhile leading business groups have all perished and their progeny are surviving by liquidating the last of their prime real estate parcels.

I shudder at such thoughts. It's easy to be indulgent with your kids. I mean, all that you own is eventually for them, right? But sometimes you have to remind yourself to be firm and teach them the value of money. Let me tell you this is not easy to do when your daughter makes puppy faces at you or your son looks crestfallen.

I remember an incident one of my friends narrated to me. Her son, still a teenager, is a competitive tennis player. He wanted to buy the latest tennis racquet, using money he had saved. 'Go ahead,' she and her husband told him. 'It's your money.'

Now, the problem was that he wanted to buy two racquets to keep one as a spare. 'But you already have four!' the parents said. He had two racquets of his own and two that had originally belonged to his elder brother. The parents stood firm. 'Why does anyone need six racquets?' they asked him.

So the saga lasted for four days. The young man spent the first day throwing a tantrum. On the second day he sulked. On the third day, he did a heavy bit of introspecting. Finally, on the fourth day he reluctantly agreed with his parents. They had a long chat and decided that he would sell two of the older racquets, and donate the other two to charity before he would go ahead with the new purchases. Case closed. My friend and her husband were happy, their son was happy. 'I hope he learned something in this process about the importance of money,' she said to me.

The Australian Actor, Errol Flynn, correctly observed something about himself that applies to all of us. He said, 'My problem lies in reconciling my gross habits with my net income.'

You are the CEO of your life

Let's dive right into it then. The very basics of expenses comprise budgeting. I'm a firm believer in treating your household expenses like that of a company. If you were managing your company's account, would you really splurge on that two-lakh-rupees sofa for the office? Here are some ways of running your life as if you were its rightful CEO.

- **Watch your bank account.** Live below your means and set money aside for investing every month. It's crucial to do this. Sophia Amoruso, the founder and owner of the mega-successful online clothing store Nasty Gal says, 'Money looks better in the bank than on your feet.' She started with used clothes and an eBay account. Now she is worth over $250 million. Think about this the next time you're going to make a spontaneous splurge.
- **Start a sinking fund.** This is simple. Open a separate savings account where you put money away for a big purchase sometime in the future. Transfer funds to this account, and forget about it. You will pat yourself on the back years later.
- **Bonuses are for saving.** It's nice to treat yourself after that nice bonus. But do you know what is nicer? Investing that money so you can grow it to treat yourself even better in the future.
- **Congratulations, you got a raise!** A naïve person will blow up that extra monthly income.

What will an intelligent person like you do? That's right, put it away and invest it.
- **Budget *all* expenses.** It's almost too easy. You're happy on payday, you plan to invest this month, eyeing some bonds or fixed deposits. Then you decide to do it over the weekend and by the time the third week of the month rolls around, you're staring in dismay at your current account. Those last-minute restaurant meals, a quick drink here and there, the designer watch you found on sale 'at a really good price'... they really do add up. Add credit card bills to this and it's a recipe for a pretty depressing end-of-month situation. Week after week, it can seem you're stuck in a vicious circle of overspending. Don't let it get out of control, there is a simple way of managing money. Budget each expense.

A budget tells your money where to go, instead of wondering where it went. It couldn't be easier. I'm from a generation that remembers writing down each expense in the cheque book. These days there is a huge array of apps and software that simplify budgeting. Use the power of technology to track and categorise all expenses against a pre-set budget. These apps can also help you set reminders and alerts for bill payments and debit limits.

Beer vs. Ferrari

A man and woman are seated in a bar and the woman watches the man washing down a couple of beers. Curious, she strikes up a conversation with him.

Woman: Do you drink beer regularly?

Man: Yes.

Woman: How many per day?

Man: Usually about three.

Woman: And how much do you pay per beer?

Man: $5 including tips.

Woman: And since how long have you been drinking beer?

Man: About twenty years, I guess.

Woman: So a beer costs $5 and you have three beers a day, which puts your spending each month at $450. In one year, it would be approximately $5,400, right?

Man: Right.

Woman: If in a year you spend $5,400, not accounting for inflation, your spending has been $108,000 in the last twenty years.

Man: What's your point?

Woman: Do you know that if you didn't drink so much beer, that money could have been put in a step-up interest savings account and after accounting for compound interest for the past twenty years, you could have now bought a Ferrari?

Man: Do you drink beer?

Woman: No.
Man: So where's your Ferrari?

The point I'm making is that you not only need to save on unnecessary expenses but also plan how those savings can be invested and applied.

The Li KaShing Model

It can be frustrating to budget without a plan, like throwing punches in the dark. The famous Hong Kong-based billionaire Li KaShing has a simple allocation model for budgeting.

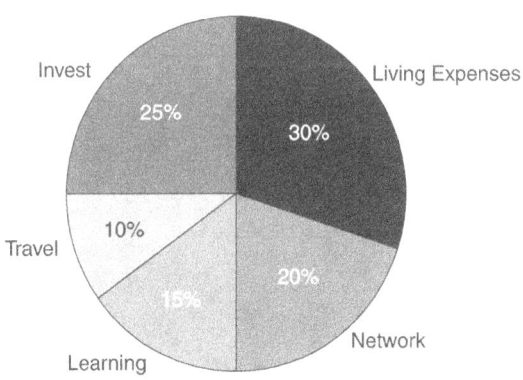

Based on this model, Li KaShing says you should spend 30% of your monthly income on living expenses,

20% on building your network, 15% on learning, 10% on travelling and invest the remaining 25%.

That sounds too abstract. Let's unravel this with an example. Say you earn Rs 1,00,000 per month. In this case, Li KaShing advises you to spend it like this:

- Rs 30,000 for living expenses.
- Rs 20,000 for making new friends and expanding your circle. In short, for networking. In the long run, networking is an important factor in your success. These expenses may include gifts, lunches you buy your friends, or just the cost of going out to meet them.
- Rs 15,000 for learning. Use this money to buy and read books, attend courses and training programs that will help you in your career or business. Never stop learning.
- Rs 10,000 for travelling. Reward yourself by travelling at least once a year. It can help one grow as a person, broaden one's horizons and develop one's outlook and instincts.
- Rs 25,000 for investing.

Obviously, the percentage allocations may vary depending upon income level. At lower income levels, a higher percentage would automatically get absorbed by living expenses whereas at very high income levels the percentage allocated for living expenses would tend to be lower.

The Frugal Buffett

Warren Buffett, consistently ranked among the world's wealthiest people, lives a frugal lifestyle. One that hasn't varied from the days before he became a billionaire. He lives in the same house in Omaha, Nebraska, that he bought in 1958 for $31,500.

His preference for McDonald's hamburgers and cherry Coke is legendary. He has never been interested in tech gadgets or luxury cars. His entertainment needs are met by watching sports on television.

Warren Buffett's annual salary is $100,000 a year at his company, Berkshire Hathaway, and the figure has not changed in twenty-five years. Buffett effortlessly manages his simple standard of living with this salary.

Buffett has been known to say 'Rule No. 1 of investing is don't lose money; Rule No. 2 is don't forget Rule No. 1.' It's a principle that he lives by and it starts by living far below his means.

So no luxury for the man? In an interview to CNBC, Buffet said, 'Success is really doing what you love and doing it well. It's as simple as that. Really getting to do what you love to do everyday – that's really the ultimate luxury. Your standard of living is not equal to your cost of living.'

When CNBC asked him what his advice to young people was, his reply was 'stay away from credit cards.'

I have put down everything I know about earning, spending and growing money in these pages.

I don't mean to lecture you. Read it, think about it, and do as you should. Your destiny, like your money, is all in your hands.

Key Takeaways

- Keep a watch on your bank account carefully.
- Start a sinking fund.
- Save and invest bonuses and raises when they happen.
- Budget all expenses (use the Li KaShing model as a reference).

Step 5

Create additional income streams

Through the years, I have seen a few cycles of economic downturn. Things get bad, they hit rock bottom, and then begins the slow process of recovery. I know many young people who were left shaken when the financial bubble burst in 2008. Of course they were traumatised. It was the first global financial crisis of their lives. It's not easy seeing friends and colleagues being handed out pink slips on an otherwise normal work morning. We spend most of our waking hours at our workplace. Love it or hate it, it starts feeling like home in our minds. And to be turned out so cruelly will leave anyone reeling.

On the other hand, it was common for our parents and grandparents to work for the same company their entire lives. In today's MNC-rich corporate landscape where the economy's fluctuations are matched by companies' attrition rates, this sounds old-fashioned and bizarre.

The fact is that generations of yore had the liberty to stay put in the same job. Security was the name of the game. But with today's volatile economy, as well as the multiple opportunities around, there are lots of exciting developments but also a high degree of uncertainty.

When you live with the possibility of having the rug pulled out from under your feet without warning, is there something you can do to bolster your financial security? Yes, two things: Create multiple sources of income, and invest. Let's go through the first of these in this chapter. We'll cover the topic of investing a little later.

Primary and secondary income

We're living in the Information Age where it's easier to start a business today than it has ever been before. And if that business involves something that you love to do, it's pure win-win, isn't it? Take the example of a friend's daughter. She is a video editor who works for an ad agency from 9 a.m. to 6 p.m. But over the weekend she dons a baker's hat and swaps her editing tools for measuring cups.

She had always loved baking for the family. We would be treated to homemade pies and muffins during parties and picnics. When she joined work and started leaving sweet treats in the office cafeteria, word of her skills spread and she started getting regular requests from colleagues for birthday cakes. Soon she set up a Facebook page and lo, a business was born!

Recently she came to me for advice about investing and I asked her if she wants to quit her job to focus on baking full time. 'No!' she exclaimed, 'If I made my hobby of baking into a job, it wouldn't be as much fun!' Well, she recently went on a European holiday with the money earned from her 'hobby', and isn't that wonderful? The trick is to come up with a successful 'side hustle' or micro business that provides an alternate source of income.

With super hectic lifestyles, people in urban India are constantly looking to outsource chores to simplify their lives. Look for gaps. Are you good with words? Professional blogging may suit you. Do your Facebook posts get a hundred likes? Is your retweet quotient going through the roof? Have you considered social media marketing? Do your quirky outfits always elicit admiring comments? Personal styling is very much in demand these days.

When setting up a side business, don't forget to brand yourself. A clear website selling your USPs and services is a must. Make yourself comfortable around technology. Digital on-demand services that could use your services are mushrooming all over. For example, TutorVista provides online tutoring via Skype, StyleCracker delivers online styling services and HolaChef is an online home-cooked meal provider.

The One-Man Company

Karsanbhai Patel completed his B.Sc. in Chemistry at age 21 and worked as a lab technician at the Geology and Mining Department of the Gujarat state Government. In 1969, Karsanbhai began selling detergent powder that he produced and packed in his backyard. This was an after-office-hours activity that he did after his day at work.

He would regularly bicycle through the neighbourhoods hawking his homemade detergent packets. The major detergent companies sold their stuff at Rs 13 per kg whereas Karsanbhai sold his at Rs 3 per kg. His soap was an instant success. Karsanbhai called his detergent 'Nirma', named after his daughter. It was only three years later that Karsanbhai chucked up his job and set up shop at a small workshop in an Ahmedabad suburb.

The Nirma brand quickly established itself in Gujarat and Maharashtra and eventually went on to revolutionize the detergent market. Nirma today is a group of companies that manufactures products ranging from cosmetics, soaps, detergents, salt, soda ash, LAB and Injectables. Today Nirma has over 15000 employees and a turnover of over Rs 3550 crores.

The point I am making is that had it not been for Karsanbhai's ingenuity in finding additional streams of income, Nirma would never have happened.

Going back to the first step where we talked about what wealth means to different people, think of these avenues not just as monetary opportunities but also options to fulfil a creative need that you never followed up on. An accountant friend of mine always dabbled with photography but his family discouraged him from becoming a full-time photographer because they felt that it may not pay well. After crunching numbers for over thirty years, he's enjoying his part-retirement but also shooting candid wedding moments for clients because he had continued to remain a part-time photographer during his working years. The money is the cherry on top.

In case any of you are feeling upset because the jobs I've spoken of so far fall in a traditional 'creative' basket, please don't be disheartened. I'm no artist or writer and yet I think I'm creative. How else would one succeed in business? My writing partner, Ashwin Sanghi, was a full-time businessman when he started writing his first book. Little did he know that one day his royalties from writing would be enough for him to live on. Amish Tripathi, the author of Shiva Trilogy, was a full-time banker while he wrote his first few books in the series. Chetan Bhagat wrote his first book while he remained an investment banker at Goldman Sachs. Similarly, Mainak Dhar, spent two decades in the corporate sector, working for Procter & Gamble and General Mills. In parallel, he is also the author of over a dozen books, some of which have been bestsellers. Sanjeev Sanyal remained as the Managing Director of Deutsche Bank while writing books on Indian history and geography.

Examine the story of Arvind Swamy. Even though he is known for his acting roles in movies such as *Roja* and *Bombay*, he has continued to work in his entrepreneurial ventures such as ProLease while acting in over twenty films. There's a dentist in Mumbai who divides her time between her clinic and a belly dancing studio each day. There's a Citibank employee who is also a rock star at night. There's an IT consultant who is also a professional photographer.

Take yet another example: that of a successful friend of mine from Ludhiana. He comes from humble stock and grew up with his government servant father and homemaker mother. When it was time for him to go to college, they borrowed money and sold family heirlooms just so that their son could study in a good university in America.

While my friend was away, his mother set up a store selling scarves to earn some extra income. The store did quite well. So she invested in a small weaving unit to design and manufacture her own products. When my friend's father retired from his job, he joined his wife's enterprise. The enterprise grew and grew and eventually my friend returned from the US to join the family business. Fast-forward twenty years and that little store is now India's largest exporter of scarves. The company employs over a thousand people, has a sophisticated manufacturing unit and sells across the globe.

When work is play

There are numerous jobs that you can do on the side. Some of these that I have come across are:
- Online tutor
- Language coach
- Blogger, columnist, writer
- Social media consultant
- Personal chef, caterer, baker
- Researcher
- App designer, web designer
- Graphic designer
- Photographer
- Astrologer
- Videographer
- Editor or proofreader
- Family archivist
- Singer, band musician
- Personal shopper, stylist
- Travel planner

- Fitness trainer
- Diet and nutrition consultant
- Pet groomer
- Artist, craftsman

The Millionaire Coach

Vinod Kumar Bansal was born in Jhansi in 1946 and graduated in mechanical engineering from the Banaras Hindu University in 1971. After graduating, he got married and moved to Kota, Rajasthan, as an engineer at JK Synthetics.

In 1974, he was diagnosed with Muscular Dystrophy. Doctors also predicted that he would have a very short lifespan. In 1981, while he was still working for JK Synthetics, he began coaching some kids in maths and science at home. He asked his wife, Neelam, to spread the word to her friends.

In 1983 he was laid off but due to sympathetic considerations Sohanlal Singhania, the owner, gave him a two year extension. But during those years between 1981 and 1985, Vinod Bansal's classes had become so popular that the income stream from that business was far more than what he was earning by way of salary.

He went on to found Bansal Classes and ended up becoming the spark that would revolutionize the Kota coaching class ecosystem. By 2008, Bansal Classes had a strength of 25,000 students and clocked an annual turnover of Rs 120 crores.

Again, it was those five years of doing parallel jobs that paved the way.

Key Takeaways

- Just because you are employed does not mean that you cannot have something else that you do in your spare time.
- Creating additional income streams will accelerate your savings and investment plan.
- Often, such 'side' activities can be the stepping stone to an entrepreneurial career.

Step 6

Harness the power of compounding

Money is a great servant but a bad master. These words are as true today as they were in the 16th century when Francis Bacon uttered them. Money is indispensable to us. Again and again I keep coming back to the same point: it is up to us to use money in a way that makes us happy. It is also entirely in our hands to fritter money away, to spend life in misery chasing money or recovering money.

I remember being asked a trick question by a Chartered Accountant once. He asked me 'What is the single creature in the world that never sleeps?' I struggled for an answer and he put me out of my misery by providing it. 'Interest,' he said. 'Even when you are asleep, the interest clock on your loan keeps ticking.' Thus, money can work round the clock to multiply or deplete itself.

The question is whether you want to master money or be mastered by it. Which brings us to the corollary to budgeting, generating additional sources of income and saving: investing.

Why invest?

Investor and fund manager, Peter Lynch, has said, 'In the long run, it's not just how much money you make that will determine your future prosperity. It's how much of that money you put to work by saving it and investing it.'

We all dream of one day owning a nice car or a fancy apartment in a high rise or just winning the lottery and putting the daily chore of earning money behind us. The difference between those who only dream and those who realise their dream is a simple trick: to find ways where you don't work for money but money works for you.

Now, if you save your money in your wallet (or lock it away in the safest vault in the world), your money will only be worth what it can buy today. But for me, money needs to be worth more. Money should generate more money.

Remember that stagnation is like death for money. Like we've already seen, if your savings are not growing at a rate that outpaces inflation, you may as well be lighting up your hard-earned cash instead of fireworks on Diwali day. It is losing value. Stamp out the fire quickly! On the other hand, if you're investing, not only are you growing your money, you are creating more of it to invest further.

Think about it. It's a rather beautiful equation: Use your money to make more money by earning interest or dividends, or on capital gains by selling assets that appreciate in value.

Take control of your life

We would all like to wake up a billionaire one morning but real life is no fantasy. Investing, on the other hand, gives you real control over your money and your destiny. I often hear young people in their twenties grumble that they don't have enough money to invest. My response to that? Nonsense. I don't believe it.

If only these people knew how much they will regret their early years when they carelessly frittered their resources away. Let me tell you what I say to them. You need to make investing a priority. Structure your budgets so you have enough left to invest.

When you invest, you are earning for your future self. This gives you chance at not only being more comfortable as life goes on, but also having more money to invest further, in effect, taking your chances at a good life ever higher.

Dave Ramsey, the famous radio show host and America's guru on money matters says, 'Financial peace isn't the acquisition of stuff. It's learning to live on less than you make, so you can give money back and have money to invest. You can't win until you do this.'

The power and beauty of compounding

Compounding is the main trait of investing. Compounding lets you earn not only on the money you are saving but also on the interest that your money is earning.

Let's understand this with a great example: the Provident Fund (or PF) account. As a salaried professional, PF can be accumulated as long as one is employed. In a way, it's an enforced discipline that helps you save. Because the PF amount is deducted from your salary by the employer, you don't even feel it and your money continues to grow over the years, reaching a substantial amount.

The PF fund is a humble avenue, but a powerful one. On maturity, it helps millions of people to buy a home, live comfortably after retirement or pay for the weddings of their children.

Life scenarios

We've finally arrived at the best part of the step, the numbers. Let's go through some scenarios of a person's wealth with and without investments.

Meet Gaurav who is twenty-three years old. Gaurav graduated with an engineering degree from a reputed college a year ago. Right off, he landed a job at a good MNC with an annual salary of Rs 8,00,000. His salary grows at an average rate of 10% per year.

Now, fast forward to Gaurav at age fifty. At this age is he wealthy? Well, the answer depends on how much he saved and how much he invested in each of the intervening twenty-seven years.

How much will Gaurav's income accumulate at the age of 50 if he...

Saves	without investing	with investing @ 12% p.a.
10%	₹1.07 Cr	₹4.2 Cr
20%	₹2.14 Cr	₹8.47 Cr
50%	₹3.2 Cr	₹12.7 Cr

Even with a mere 10% yearly savings coupled with investing, Gaurav would be worth more than 50% savings with no investments!

Robert Allen, a businessman and a member of the US Congressman once asked, 'How many millionaires do you know who have become wealthy by investing in savings accounts? I rest my case.'

Grains on a Chessboard

Once upon a time there lived a king. He was kind and generous, always taking care of the needy and rewarding wise men of the kingdom. Having heard about the king's generosity, a poor poet arrived at the king's palace. The poet recited a poem which he had written in honour of the king. Impressed by the literary talent of the poet, the king asked the poet to name his reward.

The poet pointed to the royal chess board that lay in front of the monarch and said, 'Your majesty, before you lies that chessboard of sixty-four squares. Kindly put a single grain of rice in the first square. Double that in the second square to two grains. Double that in the third square to four grains and so on until the last square. I only want that much grain from you.'

The king was surprised. 'You only want grain?' he asked the poet. 'You don't want gold or diamonds?'

'I am sure, your highness,' said the poet.

'So be it,' said the king. He gave instructions to his ministers to provide the poet with adequate grain as per his request.

An hour later, the ministers came back running to inform the monarch that there wasn't enough grain in the kingdom to meet the poet's requirement. With sixty-four squares on a chessboard, if the number of grains doubled on every successive square, then the sum of grains on all sixty-four squares would be 1 + 2 + 4 + 8 + 16 + 32 + 64 + 128 ... and so forth for the sixty-four squares. What would be the final tally? 18,446,744,073,709,551,615 grains!

That many grains would weigh 461,168,602,000 metric tons and constitute a heap of rice larger than Mount Everest!

And that, my friends, is the power of compounding.

Numbers speak the loudest

The numbers have spoken loud and clear: invest, and your money will sprint. Do not invest, and it will stay sluggish and slow.

At the end of this step, here's my challenge for you: put aside a reasonable sum regularly each month (remember the Li KaShing model that recommended 25% of your monthly budget for this) and start investing. If you're having trouble making a budget, revisit the planning step or create an additional source of income. And if you're feeling worried that you know nothing about investing, don't worry and read on.

In the coming steps we will go into the details of a variety of investment options, their pros and cons, and their various combinations that will help you create a successful investment plan.

Key Takeaway

It is only when you couple saving along with investing that the power of compounding can work for you.

Step 7

Build assets, not expenses

It's a path we're told to tread since we're young: Study hard, get a good job, save enough money, buy a car, get married, buy a house. 'Settle down,' as our parents would say. Buying your first car or your first home is often an emotional moment for people, the final brick in the tower of growing up. It proves that you're a responsible adult, taking care of your present and your future, investing in assets that will take care of your family and pay dividends for years to come.

But are all assets created equal? While reading Robert Kiyosaki's *Rich Dad, Poor Dad*, I was struck by the points he makes. 'The philosophy of the rich and the poor is this: the rich invest their money and spend what is left. The poor spend their money and invest what is left. Rich people acquire assets. The poor and middle-class acquire liabilities that they think are assets. An asset puts money in your pocket. A liability takes money from your pocket.'

So, what is an asset?

An asset is a fluid term. Narayan Murthy has famously said that his employees are his assets. You may think of your intelligence, or good looks, or your ability to make friends as your asset.

A friend of mine considers his vintage car to be his biggest asset. My logical approach to complicated matters is my asset. Another one of my friends said that his most valuable asset is his great-grandfather's watch, which was one of the few things that his parents managed to carry when they fled Pakistan at partition.

Of course, the world of finance and accounting works differently. So for the purpose of our book, anything of monetary value is an asset. This includes:
- Cash or equivalent: Physical cash, bank savings accounts, fixed deposits
- Real estate: Property, land and house
- Personal valuables: Anything that you own of value. Think jewellery, vehicles, artwork and collectibles, furniture, clothes etc.
- Investments: Stocks, bonds, mutual funds, life insurance policies, precious metals like gold, silver and so on.

What really matters

Your house is supposed to be your most valuable asset but does it generate any income for you? Not if you are staying in it. Also, your house may fetch a big amount if you were to sell it, but will you sell your house? Didn't you buy it to live in it?

So unless you bought the house with the intention of selling it in the future and making a profit on the capital gains, I'm sorry to break the news that the house you live in should not be considered as a financial asset, however high its valuation, for the simple reason that you live in it.

Assets or liabilities?

Let's examine other assets. Accounting standards classify furniture, personal computers, refrigerators, washing machines, in fact the plethora of white goods in our homes, as assets too. But as time goes by, all these appliances, even your beloved gadgets, fast lose value. Logically speaking, would you classify something that is losing value over time as an asset?

The next time you feel tempted to buy Apple's latest iPhone while an older phone rests in your pocket, keep in mind that buying the device does not increase your net worth but possibly investing in Apple stocks could. Stay aware. Remember we discussed that money is a good servant but a bad master? Consider putting your hard-earned money to work instead so it can grow.

'Assets put money in your pocket.'

The definition of a real asset for me, then, is anything that generates income now and has the potential to appreciate over time. Assets are anything that put money in your bank account.

An easy way of separating assets from liabilities is to ask yourself this: 'If I were to lose my job today, what will bring me money and what will cost me money?' Living in a fancy apartment in a beautiful location will not bring you any income. However, buying such an apartment and leasing it out can generate a steady source of rising income. Similarly, will your television or car earn you money? They will not. But a well-placed investment will. Obviously, one has to balance things in life, enjoying the moment and the fruits of your success but simultaneously ensuring that you are not getting so ahead of yourself that you stop being prudent.

So income-generating real estate, dividend-paying stocks and interest-paying bonds are assets. The banks may consider your car as an asset when they are deciding whether or not they want to give you a loan. You may even show your car as an asset in your balance sheet. But should you consider it when calculating your net-worth? The value of your brand new car goes down by 20% the second you drive it out of the showroom. Think about that.

A corollary to this idea is that if you sign up to provide rides for a service like Uber, your car does indeed become an asset because it helps you generate income. Airbnb, a service that allows homeowners to rent out their homes to travellers, helps you turn your home into a true asset, too. This also ties in with our discussions of generating additional sources of income.

Wealth is a plan for the future

The truly wealthy collect real assets while the misguided pile up liabilities. There are some exceptions, though. If you are servicing a home loan on a house for some years before it can become your own, you're most certainly living with a liability, at least in the short term. But you are working towards eventually creating a real asset, which is a good thing. Similarly, when you take an education loan to fund your engineering, law, accounting, medicine or MBA degree, you are actually investing in yourself. Your education will eventually allow you to get a job or start your own business to earn and multiply your fortunes.

What do smart people do differently? According to me, despite their present financial situation, they think long term. Even if their stars are misaligned today, they still think of the future and how to secure it. They accumulate investments that generate enough to cover their daily expenses. When you have managed to do this, you're out of the rat race and on the way to true financial freedom. Invest the extra income and see your money grow with the power and beauty of compounding.

Income and assets

So here's the bottom line. Your salary is your earned income. It's the most common type of income around the world, and it is also the most heavily taxed.

But your aim should be to collect as many appreciating assets as possible. This in turn will help you generate as much passive income as possible. Passive income is one where you don't work for it. This is true wealth. This is true freedom.

The Barber Who Owns a Rolls-Royce

The year was 1979. Nine-year-old Ramesh's father died leaving the family with nothing but a small haircutting salon. His mother worked as a domestic help to feed her son and was left with no alternative but to lease out the shop for six rupees per day.

Some years later, Ramesh dropped out of school and decided to run the salon himself. He soon realized that the income from his salon depended on his own labour hours. He needed assets that would work for him while he continued to cut hair.

He saved up money from the saloon for three years until he had enough to own a Maruti Omni. After buying the car, his mother's employer advised him to lease the car to the chipmaker Intel. It turned out to be the start of Ramesh Tours & Travels.

Today the company owns 256 luxury cars, which include a Rolls-Royce, six BMWs, nine Mercedes-Benz cars, a Jaguar, three Audis and many more. Ramesh can still be found cutting the hair of his regular customers while his assets continue to generate income for him.

Key Takeaways

- Spend money to acquire assets. Assets can help generate income, thus eventually allowing your assets to work for you.
- Anything that generates income now and has the potential to appreciate over time is an asset.
- Your aim should be to collect as many appreciating assets as possible. This in turn will help you generate as much passive income as possible.

Step 8

Make the Wealth Trinity your friend

Hinduism has always worshipped trinities. The female trinity of Lakshmi-Saraswati-Kali as well as the male trinity of Brahma-Vishnu-Shiva. Christians revere the trinity of the Father, Son and Holy Ghost. In the world of finance too, there exists a holy trinity. The trinity of:
- Risk
- Return and
- Time.

In the ensuing pages I will try to cover each element of this financial trinity in greater detail.

Risk

An American singer, Jack Yelton, quipped that 'there is a very easy way to return from a casino with a small fortune: go there with a large one.' In that sense, life is a gamble. From the slipperiness of the bathroom in the morning to the journey back home from work in the evening, every second of our life is rife with risk. Don't be fooled into believing that you're taking chances only when you buy a lottery ticket or visit a casino. Life is risky by nature and every moment is unpredictable.

Risk is inherently tied up with reward. From taming fire and domesticating wild animals to open-heart surgery and landing on the moon, some of humans' biggest feats have come from people stepping outside their comfort zone to try something different. Ancient humans hunted to survive. Predators and the vagaries of merciless nature constantly endangered their lives. Every morning they had two choices: go out to hunt (with the risk of being eaten alive), or starve to death in their cave shelters. We all know which option our ancestors chose.

That brings me to financial risk. You may be surprised to know that financial risk is not a modern concept. In fact, humans have been dabbling in this for over six thousand years.

The people of the Indus Valley Civilisation sailed through choppy seas to visit Mesopotamia and Egypt for trade. As far back as 400 BCE, Gujarati traders regularly travelled to South East Asia, carrying cotton, gold and spices. These ancient entrepreneurs bet their fortunes on an unpredictable journey aboard rudimentary ships across vast distances and time.

Shipwrecks were common, as were pirate attacks. There was risk of disease, starvation, getting lost. But they persisted because the rewards—returns of 2,000 times the investment—compensated for the risk.

If you read Chanakya's *Arthashastra*, you will find that 2300 years ago he had prescribed the interest rates that could be charged for extending loans of various types:
- Normal transactions 1.25% per month (15% p.a.)
- Commercial transactions 5% per month (60% p.a.)
- Risky travel through forests for trade 10% per month (120% p.a.)
- Risky travel by sea for trade 20% per month (240% p.a.)

You can clearly see that Kautilya knew that higher risks justified higher rewards.

We've come a long way from the days of our ancestors. Taking risk no longer translates to losing our life, at least not literally. But it's still the same primeval game, only in a different form. Because today we play with risk via the markets.

In the world of finance, risk is usually measured as the degree of uncertainty in an expected outcome. Risk is the possibility of losing some, or all, of the original investment.

Determining your risk appetite can be tricky. Of course, risk tolerance differs from person to person. It is tied to your income, lifestyle, goals and approach to life. While one might believe that younger folks may be willing to take more risk than the older generation or that the less wealthy may be more risk averse, I have in fact seen many instances of the exact opposite.

In this step and beyond, we'll read about not only protecting ourselves from risk but also manipulating risk for higher returns.

In order to meet the increasing financial requirements of daily life and maintain a good standard of living, we not only need to save money, but also need to invest it in avenues where one can get maximum returns. However, as the return expectations increase, so does the risk. In that sense, risk and return are two sides of the same coin.

Tragedies occur when people take risk without being aware that they are taking a risk. My philosophy is that investing smartly is more about knowing the risks than the returns. Make no mistake: It's entirely your responsibility to figure out what kind of risk each investment entails, and whether you're willing to take it on. No investment advisor will ever highlight all the risks to you transparently.

The Million Idlis Man

P. C. Mustafa failed in Class 6. His family lived in a remote part of Kerala and was exceedingly poor. His father was a coolie. Mustafa picked himself up and tried harder. He eventually managed to join an engineering programme at the National Institute of Technology, Calicut. He soon found himself employed at Motorola which sent him to the UK for a project.

He missed his family, food and festivals. He soon kicked up the Motorola job and went to the Middle East and worked for Citibank for the next seven years. He eventually left his technology job with Citi and returned to India and pursued an Executive MBA at IIM Bangalore.

On weekends during his IIM stint, Mustafa would sit at a kirana shop that was run by his cousins. He noticed that women from all economic sections would drop in to buy batter for idlis or dosas. The stuff would literally fly off the shelves. An idea was born and he dipped into his savings of Rs 14 lakhs to fund it, taking a massive risk at the time.

Mustafa and his cousins bought 5,000 kg of rice and made 15,000 kg of batter. They distributed this batter as samples to the women customers. During the course of that experiment they ended up getting vital feedback on how the ideal batter should be made. They soon rented a fifty-square-feet kitchen, bought a grinder and a scooter and ID Special Foods Pvt Ltd. was born.

ID Special Foods today sells in eight cities: Bangalore, Mangalore, Mysore, Mumbai, Chennai, Hyderabad, Pune and Sharjah. 200 Tata delivery trucks go around each city delivering fresh batter to shops. ID employs

650 people, who distribute to 10,000 stores a day. The amount of batter it sells in one day can make a million idlis. The turnover of the company is over Rs 100 crores.

But would it ever have happened without that initial risk taken by Mustafa?

Personally, I learned about risk the hard way. After I sold one of our ventures, I had some capital to invest. I hired a few big name banks to advise me on the right portfolio strategy. Their advisors were suave, glib and full of jargon. They built castles in the sky for me and I bought them. Why wouldn't I? They sold themselves as the experts and I took them at face value. In hindsight, I was making decisions without knowing all the facts about the product, my risk appetite and the suitability of the portfolio. You can guess what happened next. The hotshot advisors made money. I did not. This series of many unfortunate outcomes eventually taught me that I had failed to assess the risk of each investment option.

Risk rarely announces itself. Rather, you have to dig around for it. Return on the other hand is easy to sell and easy to understand. I promised myself that I would never let smooth-talking bankers outsmart me. That's when I threw myself into studying everything about investments.

With time, not only did I recover my losses but managed to grow the capital at a handsome rate. And here is what I learnt: the notion that all wealthy people are well informed is a fallacy. When glib advisors swoop over you and floor you with verbiage, you might feel pressured to agree with everything they say because either you don't want to look stupid or because you may not have enough information to question them.

Therefore, before such a situation arises, do your homework. This is why I have written this book, so that you can learn from my mistakes. Look, you've worked hard to make your money and save it. You will perhaps need to work harder to manage it. Money cannot manage itself.

Looking back, I can tell you that deciding how much and what type of risks to take is critical to your investment returns. Like the early humans, if you bar yourself from all risk, you will also close the door to earning returns. On the other hand, exposing yourself to a high degree of risk that you don't understand can make your losses spiral out of control. The key lies in making the right choices. So let's take a look at different kinds of risks, ways of measuring them, and methods for managing risk.

Don't try this at home!
Ramkrishna Dalmia grew up in poverty in Calcutta during the 1930s. He was just twenty-two when his father died and had to support seven family members all living in a single room, the rent of which was Rs 13 per month.

Dalmia was confident, brash and in a hurry. He wanted to make money quickly. He speculated in silver, lost badly, and ended up defaulting on debts. He was declared insolvent and soon, no one in the market wanted to have any dealings with him.

One day he received a cable from London indicating that the price of silver was about to go up. Dalmia ran over to the bazaar and pleaded with his business acquaintances to buy silver, but to no avail. His reputation was such that no one would do business with him.

Dejected, Dalmia went to the house of a wealthy astrologer. It was the same astrologer who had predicted that Dalmia would become fabulously wealthy one day. The astrologer agreed to buy silver worth 7,500 pounds from Dalmia. Dalmia rushed to the General Post Office to send off a cable for the purchase.

While he was taking a dip in the Ganges the next day, Dalmia got to know that the astrologer had backed out of the transaction. He returned home to find a cable confirming his purchase transaction. He now owned metal but had no buyer. In addition, there was news that the market had declined.

Silver prices, however, rebounded over the next few days. Given that Dalmia had not settled his holdings, he realized that he had made a substantial profit. Any careful businessman would have booked the profit but Dalmia was not one of those. His appetite for risk was enormous.

He quietly took his wife's only piece of jewellery, pawned it, and placed a fresh bet through another broker for 10,000 pounds worth of silver. Silver prices rose yet again and he doubled his capital. He used this to buy even more silver until he had made his profits multiply seven times.

Dalmia then cabled the brokers to book profits but the cable got corrupted during transmission. In the meantime, the market rose again brilliantly. By the time that Dalmia actually liquidated his position, his profits were fifteen times his capital. He had become an exceedingly rich man and he laid the foundation of a massive industrial empire using that capital. But remember that he had been on the verge of losing everything with that first silver trade.

Why did I narrate this story to you? Simply to illustrate that risk appetite varies widely across individuals and that it often works in mysterious ways.

The world of finance is filled with gobbledygook. Its lingo can often confuse and unsettle investors. Do not feel overwhelmed. As long as you have your wits about you and your common sense intact, you will understand the concepts that follow easily.

There are many ways of measuring risk and each risk measure is unique. We'll go through some of these fundamental terms which I believe are the most important to understand. If it starts to seem tiring, remember one thing: a little sweating to understand the principles of risk is much better than throwing your hard-earned money into a wishing-well and 'hoping' for the best. You should also feel free to explore the Internet. In particular, investopedia.com is a great online resource where you can find answers to almost all of your doubts.

- **Standard deviation** (δ): Standard deviation is used by investors as a gauge for the amount of expected volatility. Let's take an example. There are two stocks: Company A and Company B. Both are priced at Rs 100. A year later, both the stocks are at Rs 120, i.e. a 20% return. At first glance, it would appear that both stocks are the same in terms of performance. Now consider this: through the year, Company A shares touched a high of 115 and a low of 90, thus trading in a Rs 25 band from its starting point. Company B, however, touched a high of 130 and a low of 80, thus trading in a band of Rs 50 from its starting point. Which one would you prefer? Company A, which appears to be slow and steady, or Company B, which was clearly more volatile through the year? Standard deviation is simply a measure of how much an investment's returns vary in comparison to its mean. This is useful because it helps you gauge how steady a fund's returns have been over a period of time. So if a fund gives an

average of 8% yearly returns with a standard deviation of 4%, you can expect your returns to vary between 4% and 12%.
- **Beta (β):** Beta is the systemic risk of an investment in comparison to the market as a whole. The market is represented by a leading stock market index (the Nifty or Sensex in India). The beta of the market is always 1.0. A beta of 1.0 indicates that the security's price will move perfectly in sync with the market. A beta of less than 1.0 means that the security will be less volatile than the market. A beta of greater than 1.0 indicates that the security's price will be more volatile than the market. For example, if a stock's beta is 1.20, it's theoretically 20% more volatile than the market.
- **Alpha (α):** Alpha is the measure of the performance on a risk-adjusted basis. The excess return of the security or fund relative to the return of the benchmark index is a fund's alpha. A simple way to think about this is that if the Sensex returns 15% annually over a two-year period, and your portfolio manager is able to generate 17% over the same period, the excess return or Alpha over the Sensex is 2% per year. The Alpha, therefore, is a measure of the portfolio manager's skill in being able to beat the benchmark.

So when comparing investment returns, don't just look at the absolute numbers, but also how much risk was involved in generating those returns.

Return

Having understood the fundamentals of risk, let's turn our attention to return. It is absolutely critical to understand that one return is different from another.

One can often be fooled into believing that the return on a proposed investment is far higher than what it actually is. The reason for this is that the word 'return' can be seen in various ways:

- **Absolute Return:** Let's say you invest Rs 100. Six months later it is worth Rs 120. Your Absolute Return is Rs 20 or 20%.
- **Annualised Return:** The Absolute Return adjusted for twelve months. Taking the example above, the Absolute Return was 20% over six months. It means that the return over twelve months would be 40%.
- **Compounded Annual Growth Rate (CAGR):** Let's say you invested Rs 100 and made Rs 40 in the first year, Rs 50 in the second year and Rs 60 in the third year. At what constant rate of growth would your Rs 100 become Rs 250 over three years? The answer is 35.72%. How? If I invested Rs 100 at a

CAGR of 35.72%, then it would become Rs 135.72 at the end of the first year, Rs 184.20 by the end of the second year and Rs 250 by the end of the third year.

- **Internal Rate of Return (XIRR):** The annualised return over an extended period of time for a set of cash flows that could happen over varying time intervals. I will not go into the technicalities but XIRR is simply an easy way to compare two or more investments even though the time periods and inflow-outflow patterns may vary.

It is a common mistake to consider a large Absolute Return as a great return. Refer to the table below to see how a two-times return on investment over a ten-year timeframe (common in certain illiquid investments such as real estate, venture capital etc.) actually translates into only a 7% annualised return that doesn't even beat inflation.

	Annualised Returns			
Absolute Returns	3 years	5 years	7 years	10 years
2x Original Investment	26%	15%	10%	7%
3x Original Investment	44%	25%	17%	12%
7x Original Investment	91%	48%	32%	21%

Time

So far, we have established what risk is. Simply, the possibility of losing your hard-earned money. We have also explained that not every return is the same. That depends on the definition of return that one applies. The relationship between risk and return is often characterised in terms of give and take. You may have heard the phrase 'high risk, high return,' implying that the more risk you take, the greater your return. Not only is this often incorrect, but also misleading. There are no such guarantees. Just as high risk means the possibility of higher returns, it also means higher potential losses.

What's more, in reiterating this common misconception, people ignore a key factor. Time. The wealthiest of people did not build their fortunes overnight. Enter, the third element of the trinity: time.

American money-advisor, Dave Ramsey, says that 'building wealth is a marathon, not a sprint.' Return and time are joined at the hip. When you have a long-term investment like land, even when it underperforms, the temptation to pull it out is low because the investment is illiquid. The danger of rash decisions comes with liquidity.

When stock markets tumble, it can be incredibly hard to resist selling. Human nature tends to jump to the worst conclusions, and during bad times it can be difficult to shake away the feeling that things will only get worse. On the other hand, when the markets are rising, many investors' fear of missing out tempts them to buy even though this means that they might be entering the markets at a very expensive price. So in both such situations, take a deep breath, and hold on.

The Value of Patience

India's big bull and best-known stock market investor is Rakesh Jhunjhunwala. An analysis carried out by Mint in 2015 showed that his highest returns were on stocks that he had held for at least ten years.

An analysis of eighty-four companies in which Rakesh Jhunjhunwala held at least a 1% stake found that he held his investments for an average of 3.44 years. In contrast, the average holding tenure for equity mutual funds did not exceed two years.

In some companies such as Titan and Lupin, he has held his stakes for ten years or more. He has maintained his stake in fifteen other companies for between five and ten years.

The analysis showed that his average returns were highest from the stocks he held the longest. The average absolute return on stocks he held for at least ten years was a staggering 3271.52% while the average return on stocks he held for less than a year was 9.23%.

Take my word that if you watch your money on a daily basis, you are bound to get nervous and do something rash. I have seen people panicking and selling out during volatile periods. This is a grave and expensive mistake because you will not be in the market to make money when it rebounds.

Consider someone who invested in the boom year of 2007. During the financial crisis of 2008, she saw her portfolio fall by 50%. She panicked and sold her securities. Not only did she incur a permanent loss of capital, she is unlikely to invest in the equity markets again. She has to now either compromise on her lifestyle or work longer hours for years to make up for her folly.

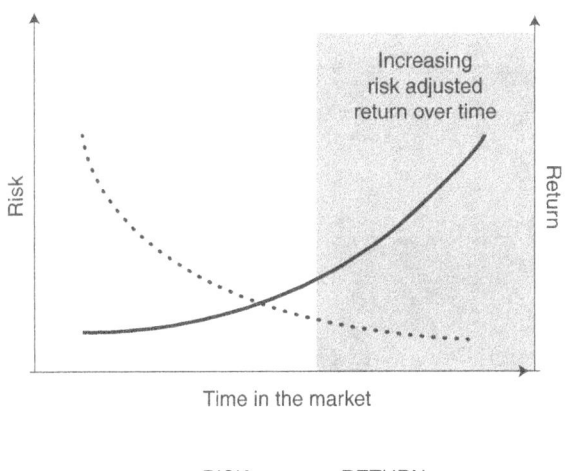

Historically, some of the worst short-term market losses have given way to substantial market recovery. Always, I repeat, always remember that *time in the market is much more important than timing the market.*

How much time do you have?

This brings us to another set of confusing words: risk-adjusted returns over time. But all it means is that before you make an investment, you must determine the amount of time you have to keep your money invested. Along with your financial goals, risk appetite and financial situation, keep in mind your time horizon, which is the number of years before you start using your returns.

		Annualised Returns (%)						
Month (June)	SENSEX	1 year	3 years	5 years	7 years	10 years	12 years	15 years
2000	4453							
2001	3558	−20.12						
2002	3161	−11.15						
2003	3182	0.66	−10.6					
2004	4818	51.42	10.64					
2005	6749	40.08	28.76	8.67				
2006	10451	54.86	48.65	24.05				

2007	14571	39.42	44.61	35.75	18.45			
2008	15963	9.55	33.24	38.06	23.92			
2009	14871	−6.84	12.47	25.28	24.76			
2010	17022	14.47	5.32	20.33	27.07	14.35		
2011	18376	7.96	4.81	11.95	21.08	17.84		
2012	15965	−13.12	2.39	1.84	13.09	17.58	11.23	
2013	19610	22.83	4.83	4.2	9.41	19.94	15.29	
2014	24859	26.76	10.6	10.82	7.93	17.83	18.75	
2015	26837	7.96	18.9	9.53	7.7	14.8	19.45	12.72
Instances of Negative Returns		**4**	**1**	**0**	**0**	**0**	**0**	**0**

	Time Period						
	1 year	3 years	5 years	7 years	10 years	12 years	15 years
Loss Probability %	**27**	**8**	**NIL**	**NIL**	**NIL**	**NIL**	**NIL**
Standard Deviation %	24	18	12	8	2	4	0

As is clear from the table, the longer you hold an investment, the lower the probability of a negative return. The caveat is that you should be holding a fundamentally good investment. We will discuss what a 'good' investment is later in this book.

Let me explain with an example. If you have five lakhs to invest today but will need it in a year to buy a car, investing in high-risk stocks may not be the best idea. You may be forced to sell your stocks at a loss.

However, if you're planning to invest your five lakhs towards your child's wedding, which you will need after twenty years, by all means invest in higher-risk options because you do not need to react to short-term market volatility. Of course, if you've bought a good-for-nothing investment, you will not make money no matter how long you wait for. But generally the longer you hold on to something good, the probability of it giving a negative return goes down. The cycles play themselves out. There is more time to recover the losses and give higher returns.

Think about this. Sachin Tendulkar started playing cricket at the age of sixteen. By age twenty-nine, he had already amassed over 12,000 runs in one-day matches. On the other hand, Robin Singh joined the Indian team at the age of twenty-five and retired twelve years later. He could manage only 2,336 runs in one-day matches. What exactly am I trying to tell you? Simple. The earlier you start investing, the greater the odds that you would end up making more money. And remember one thing. Runs scored in cricket don't multiply automatically but investment does!

In light of this, when investing, it may help to divide your time horizon into buckets:

- **Short-term time horizon (Less than two years to invest):** Low risk investments such as fixed income instruments.

- **Medium-term time horizon (Three to five years to invest):** Mix of equities and fixed income based on your risk appetite.
- **Long-term time horizon (More than five years):** Considerably higher proportion of equities.

In summary, I must remind you that rewards come to you when you take a chance. Often while travelling to a new country, I see many people hesitant to try something new. In Paris, I have seen many Americans making a beeline for a McDonald's and Indians looking for a curry house. I always like to go to a local bistro and order something unfamiliar. There have been times when my dish has turned out to be bland or inedible. But this is also how I discovered some amazing dishes that ordinarily I wouldn't have known about.

I must add that when it comes to financial matters, the more informed you are, the better you will be able to evaluate the risks and returns. Is it possible to prepare for risks? Yes it is. For a smart portfolio, diversification is of utmost importance. The right investment mix will help you get the balance between risk and return. In simple terms: Don't put all your eggs in one basket.

Key Takeaways

- The wealth trinity consists of risk, return and time.

- Risk is usually measured as the degree of uncertainty in an expected financial outcome.
- Some of the measures of risk are Standard Deviation, Beta and Alpha.
- Return also has different meanings. Absolute return, annualised return, CAGR and IRR are different ways to look at return.
- Often, you may find yourself misled by a high absolute return even though the annualized return or CAGR is far lower.
- You should divide your time horizon into short-term, medium-term and long-term when looking at investment options.
- There is no substitute for time and patience in the world of investing.
- Time in the market is more important than timing the market.

Step 9

Have an asset allocation strategy

Here we are, finally, at the heart of the matter. Asset allocation is at the centre of your investment strategy. If you're new to the world of investing, if you've just started working and are thinking about long term plans for investments: Welcome. I'm excited to see you here.

The fact that you're still reading this book means that you are well aware that the days of storing money in a tea jar or shoving it under the mattress are gone. So let's talk shop. Remember how in the initial pages of this book we discussed how wealthy you would like to be? This is the other half of that puzzle: how to reach that financial goal.

In his 1973 bestseller, *A Random Walk Down Wall Street*, Burton Malkiel wrote that a blindfolded monkey throwing darts at a newspaper's financial pages could select a portfolio that would do just as well as one carefully selected by experts. Subsequent studies by researchers have shown that the portfolios chosen by simulated dart-throwing monkeys have usually resulted in portfolios that often outperformed the market. Less-developed primates, it would seem, are better at picking stocks than humans. And it is precisely for this reason that I think that you should spend more time on asset allocation rather than stock picking.

You may have heard people talk about investments using many complicated words. Many people think investing is about buying stocks or mutual funds or about 'playing the market'. You may feel nervous or inadequate, and may be put off by the sheer incomprehensibility of the whole task. But investing is the best and only way of making your money work for you. It's the simplest way to grow your money over time.

You don't need an MBA or a master's degree in finance to start investing. Tell me, do you need to be Sachin Tendulkar to hit a cricket ball with a bat? Do you need to be Gordon Ramsey to make a simple cup of tea? Of course not. So read these pages, then go ahead and hit that ball.

Investing is not just about stocks. Investments are multi-layered instruments with varying degrees of risks and returns. And it's up to you to find the right combination of investments for yourself. Trust me, there is no magic formula here and barely any rights and wrongs.

Some people like watching action films and get a kick out of horror movies. Some people go for family or romantic stories, while others prefer more cerebral ones. One person's *Hum Aapke Hain Kaun* is another person's *Sholay*. Similarly, asset allocation is a subjective mix, like your personality.

Take another example. A friend of yours may be into adventure travel, scoping out bungee jumping and rappelling wherever she goes. On the other hand, another friend's perfect vacation may be all about chilling while he relaxes on a beach, shops and frequents fancy restaurants. There is no right or wrong way to vacation. Whatever works for you works for you.

In the same way, your asset allocation is unique to you and don't let anyone else tell you otherwise. The pages coming up will help you determine the right asset allocation for yourself, and assist you in avoiding any rookie mistakes.

The magic of the market

There are many ways of participating in the markets: equity, fixed income, commodities, real estate and so on. Don't be put off by these words because in forthcoming steps I'll explain what each of them means.

Now, in the previous chapter I was telling you about my bad experience with the jargon-filled speak of financial advisors and how I rejected a lot of it. You may say, 'Hey, why are you throwing bits of jargon at us now? Isn't "asset allocation" just another fancy phrase?' Please hear me out. Asset allocation is not a complicated cocktail of financial jargon. It's simply putting your money to work in the best place in a well-thought mix. In fact, it's a proven fact that determining your asset allocation is more important than the individual investments you buy. Take a second to absorb that fact.

I'm not making this up. In 1986, three researchers, Brinson, Hood and Beebower, showed in their landmark paper that over 90% of your portfolio's risk-adjusted return is connected to your asset allocation. This finding rocked the finance world.

What exactly is asset allocation?

Asset allocation refers to the collection of investments you own. A good portfolio has a diverse selection of uncorrelated investment types, which are called asset classes.

'Uncorrelated, say what?' you might exclaim. Let me introduce the concept of uncorrelated investments here. If you invest in different instruments that are all tied to the same market risks (for example, direct stocks and equity mutual funds which have the same direct stocks in their fund), chances are that these investments will rise and fall with the market in the same time frame and proportion. This is for the simple reason that they are correlated.

So even though you may think you have spread your investments, you have actually not diversified the risk. For this reason, your asset allocation programme must include investing in uncorrelated assets to even out market risks across your portfolio. It's like having a solid Rahul Dravid alongside a swashbuckling Virendra Sehwag in your team!

Diversification balances risk

John Templeton, a British stock investor and philanthropist famously said, 'The only investors who shouldn't diversify are those who are right one hundred per cent of the time.' I would trust John Templeton, a man who *Money* magazine called 'the greatest global stock picker of the century'. He was a fascinating chap, an alumni of Oxford and Yale, where he financed his tuition with winnings from poker tournaments.

So let's get real. No one is right a hundred per cent of the time. Not you, not the people whose job it is to play the market, not even the greatest stock picker in the world. In fact, each time that one investor sells, another investor buys, and they both think they're smart!

Now, people can be very random about asset allocation. Granted, there is no set recipe for it. But if you're on the extreme spectrum where you're going, 'Little bit of this, little bit of that,' without pausing to think of what you're creating, you're bound to end up with a dish that tastes pretty bad.

It's important to understand how diversification works. In fact, you know what? You already know how it works because you have seen it play out in everyday life without ever having dabbled in stocks.

Think about what you ate for your meal yesterday. Most likely, it would have been a combination of carbohydrates (rice, roti), vitamins and minerals (green vegetables), and protein (daal, poultry, fish or meat). This is a balanced diet because each component plays a specific role for your body. Similarly, diversification is spreading your money amongst different kinds of investments so that if one loses money, the others make up for the loss. And in aggregate, in the long term they are all appreciating and beating inflation.

In other words, it reiterates the age-old maxim of not putting all your eggs in one basket. By investing in various asset classes, you are reducing the risk of losing money. Since different investment categories are affected by different types of market conditions, by diversifying your portfolio you are reducing the risk of fluctuations or volatility of market returns and therefore protecting yourself from losses.

How to get started

OK, let's do this. You're ready to understand and create your own balanced asset allocation plan. I'm going to go into some key factors to consider before you determine an asset allocation model that is right for you.

You, the reader, may be over-eager or very patient by nature, but one common factor amongst all of you is this: your asset allocation plan should be able to ride out the storms of economic downturns (we've had two since 2000 already) and grow your money steadily by harnessing the power of compounding.

In other words, your asset allocation should be a mix of uncorrelated investments which will help you meet your financial goals at a level of risk you're comfortable with. Here are some points to help you determine your allocation:
- Determine your time horizon
- Determine your allocation
- Understand your risk appetite
- Know yourself
- Ask the right questions: Which asset class, not which product
- Know why you own it

- Consider Time vs. Product
- Ask yourself: 'Should I try to time the markets?'
- Regularly rebalance and review
- Sell high, buy low

These are explained in detail below:

Determine your time horizon

Asset allocation has a very, very important effect on whether you will meet your financial goals or not. For this, it's important to consider how long you're going to invest for. Your time horizon is the number of years before you start needing to use your returns. This is important because your patterns of savings and consumption vary as you grow up and move through life's phases.

- **Long-term time horizon:** For investors who have a long time to retirement, a portfolio with 80% to 90% in equity and 10% to 20% in fixed income is said to be an ideal mix. A long-term investment horizon can tolerate short-term volatility in the stock market.
- **Short-term time horizon:** However, for someone who is approaching retirement, it is advisable to have a more balanced mix of equity and fixed income in their portfolio, say 50:50 split between equities and fixed income.

Generally, it's better to gradually reduce your percentage of long-term investments as you come closer to the end of your investment time horizon. This way you can avoid the unfortunate risk of having to sell your investments at a time when the markets are down. During the financial crisis of 2008, many people nearing retirement lost their life's savings when the markets crashed because a majority of their asset allocation comprised stocks. A big, sad mistake. When it was finally time for them to cash out their life's investments, boom! The market fluctuation wiped them out.

Determine your allocation

A classic rule of thumb is that the percentage of equity in your portfolio can be calculated by subtracting your age from 100 i.e. Percentage of equity in your portfolio = 100 – Your age.

So if you're thirty years old, you should keep 70% of your portfolio in stocks. And if you're seventy, you should keep 30% of your portfolio in stocks. This is the simplest way to determine your allocation. Of course, having only one rule of thumb is dangerous because it implies that only age determines risk tolerance. We know that's not true. There are more sophisticated asset allocation models but really, this is a great starting point. Read on to know the remaining factors.

Understand your risk appetite

Let's face it. Financial markets are unpredictable. In the last fifteen years since 2000, the world has already seen two recessions, both of which caused drops of 50% or more in the market. Many people's lives were ruined. So my advice is not to be caught unaware. How? By profiling for risk.

It's true that all investments come with some degree of risk. That's a given. But we read earlier that risk and return often go hand in hand. So if you don't include enough risk in your asset allocation, your investments may not earn enough to meet your financial goals. At the same time, if you include too much risk, you may be left with no money at all. What is one to do?

A great way to gauge your tolerance for risk and losses is to test your portfolio to see how it would have performed through a number of scenarios.

By looking at the performance of certain asset allocation strategies over time, you can determine how the losses and gains over these cycles would have made you feel. This way, you can get a better handle on your investment decisions if similar circumstances arise in the future.

Here are some statistics on how different strategies look against each other going back to the year 2001.

Return profile: 1st January 2001 to 1st January 2015					
	100% Equity	70% Equity, 30% Fixed Income	50% Equity, 50% Fixed Income	30% Equity, 70% Fixed Income	100% Fixed Income
Initial Investment (₹)	1,00,000	1,00,000	1,00,000	1,00,000	1,00,000
Final Value (₹)	6,60,448	5,56,302	4,72,415	3,85,923	2,65,063
Absolute Return	560%	456%	372%	286%	165%
CAGR	14.43%	13.03%	11.72%	10.12%	7.21%
Highest Monthly Return	23.97%	16.89%	12.17%	7.45%	0.90%
Lowest Monthly Return	−22.96%	−15.82%	−11.06%	−6.30%	0.27%
Highest Annual Gain	73.82%	53.16%	39.39%	25.61%	9.50%
Lowest Annual Gain	−50.63%	−32.77%	−20.87%	−8.96%	4.39%
Equity: Nifty					
Fixed Income: HDFC Liquid Fund, Growth Option					
NAV Source: ACE Mutual Fund					

So had you invested Rs 1,00,000 on January 1, 2001, this is what the returns would be over a fourteen-year period, given different asset allocation strategies: An investment of Rs 1,00,00 on January 1, 2001 would have been worth Rs 6,60,448 if it was only invested in equity. A portfolio of only fixed income, on the other hand, would have resulted in Rs 2,65,063.

As is clear, equities far outperformed fixed income in this time frame. The returns are higher but by now we have discussed it enough for you to know that the volatility and fluctuations are higher, too.

To earn this higher return in equities you would have had to stomach some significant notional losses through this period. If you refer to the table, with a 100% equity portfolio there was a year in which you would have lost 50.63% of the value. On the other hand, while the 100% fixed income portfolio has been steady and has not seen a negative year, the CAGR is actually lower than the average inflation rate through the period!

Lesson learned? Gains are higher in an equity-concentrated portfolio but the losses are smaller in a fixed-income portfolio.

Know yourself

Remember the joke about the psychiatrist who asks his patient if he has difficulty in making decisions?

The patient answers, 'Well, doctor, yes and no.' Life is all about choices and we've all struggled with them. Do you want cornflakes or *dosa* for breakfast? The crossword or television on Sunday? Understanding the decisions you make and why you make those decisions is critical in asset allocation.

I hope that by now you would say to yourself: 'My mix of assets has to strike a balance between my desire for comfort now, and my desire for comfort in the future.'

The reward for taking on more risk is the possibility of a higher return. So if you have a longer time horizon, it makes sense to invest in assets like stocks and bonds that have a greater risk. With time, the volatility in the return is tempered down. On the other hand it's better to invest in cash investments for a short-term time horizon. I'll explain more on cash investments in the next step.

Ask the right questions: which asset class, not which product

Let's go back to Brinson and his colleagues' findings about asset allocation and its relationship with returns and volatility. They showed that active investment decisions such as security selection and market-timing play minor roles when compared to the role of asset allocation.

By allocating your investments to broader asset classes, you can easily diversify your risks, if not remove them. The best way to offset volatility is to have countering and uncorrelated asset classes (like stocks and bonds) in one portfolio. We'll go into the details of these asset classes in later steps.

Know why you own it

Everything in your portfolio must be there for a reason. Many people assume that having a large number of funds means they're diversified. What they fail to take into account is how the individual parts work with each other to create the perfect whole. So here's what I say: always think of how your individual holdings work within the construct of an overall portfolio and investment plan.

If you feel you don't know enough to do this, let me tell you, admission of your lack of knowledge here is the ultimate sign of intelligence. Read on, make yourself aware, and make the right decision. A complex investment world does not require a complex response. In the world of investments, simplicity is the ultimate sophistication.

Consider Time vs. Product

Consider the fact that with any investment, you need to choose an asset to invest in (let's call it 'product') and you also need to make that decision at a given point in time. Let's examine the outcomes:

	Wrong Product	Right Product
Right Time	✗	✓
Wrong Time	✗	✗

As common sense tells us, Right Time-Right Product is clearly the best combination and Wrong Time-Wrong Product is certainly the worst. But there is a caveat. It's possible that the wrong product at the right time gives better returns than the right product at the wrong time. What I'm trying to say is that it is important not just to consider the financial product, but also the bigger economic conditions that will impact the right time to make the investment.

Let's take an example. If you had invested into a mutual fund like HDFC Equity Fund during the lows of March 2009, the outcome would have been very positive over the next twelve months. In effect, Right time-Right Product. Now, assume that you had invested in the HDFC Equity fund in January 2008. While HDFC Equity is a consistent performer in the large cap mutual fund space, investing in January 2008 at the peak of equity markets would still have led to losses over the next twelve months because of the financial crisis that followed. Now, this was not a fault of the product but a result of market behaviour. Hence, Wrong Time-Right Product.

Ask yourself: 'Should I try to time the markets?'

In October 2008, Warren Buffett wrote an opinion piece for the *New York Times* which carried the lines that have now become so famous, they can be considered a principle: 'Be fearful when others are greedy, and be greedy when others are fearful.'

Warren Buffet is often claimed to be a 'bottom-up' investor who does not time the market. However, he has an amazing track record of reacting to the markets to gain from the market movements. What are we to make of Buffet's actions? The simplicity of his logic is spelled out in his quote above. Buffet's philosophy is to buy equity for cheap when others are fearful and the markets are down. And then to sell when the markets are overvalued and people are greedy. He simply believes in selling an overvalued stock and buying it back when the prices are more reasonable.

This is not to say that investors should have a trading mindset. This example tells us to be aware of major cycles in the market and to definitely avoid the opposite behaviour at all costs, which is to buy high and sell low which is a surefire way to lose money.

Feeling confused? There is a method to this madness. Let me explain it in the next point about rebalancing.

Regularly rebalance and review

Periodic rebalancing and review is key to successful investing. Don't be confused by the term. Many people hear of rebalancing all the time but aren't quite sure when or how to do it.

It's simple. Rebalancing is bringing your portfolio back to your original asset allocation. Most of the time, some investments end up growing faster than others. For example, you have a portfolio of Rs 100. Of this, Rs 40 is invested in equity and Rs 60 in fixed income. Two years later your equity component has appreciated to Rs 65 and your fixed income has also appreciated (albeit slower) to Rs 65. In effect, the portfolio which was original 40:60 between equity and fixed income is now 50:50.

Over time, this gap in growth rates makes your investments deviate from your financial goals. The investments that are doing well take up more of your portfolio than those that are slower. This is not aligned with your asset allocation, which you had determined based on the amount of risk you're comfortable with. By rebalancing, you can return your portfolio to its original balance.

Let's say you determine that you will have an asset allocation of 70% equity and 30% fixed income. Recently, due to a stock market boom, stocks go up to make 90% of your portfolio. In this case, you should either sell some of your equity investments or buy more of the under-weighted fixed income categories to restore the asset allocation balance.

A periodic review of your holdings is equally important. If there is a position in your portfolio which has been a laggard in terms of performance, you should replace it with a better alternative. While we are long-term investors, a periodic review and rebalance mechanism can add a lot of value. This way no category will have any extra weightage and your portfolio will not be dependent on the success of one particular investment or asset class.

Sell high, buy low

Going back to Buffett's trick of 'timing' the markets, your asset allocation strategy will be your guide that tells you what to invest in and when. So while the herd is selling stocks while markets are falling and buying stocks when markets are rising, all you have to do is to make sure your portfolio is balanced, which will automatically make you sell when high and buy when low. This would be in perfect accord with Buffett's dictum of 'Be fearful when others are greedy, and be greedy when others are fearful.'

Finally, remember this: like your diet, your portfolio should have an optimal mix of assets. My hope for you is to have an asset allocation which is healthy and beneficial. I hope your returns grow, your risks are minimised, and you prosper.

Key Takeaways

- Asset allocation is simply putting your money to work in the best place in a well-thought mix.
- A mix should allow for diversification thus reducing risk.
- Determine your time horizon while deciding an asset allocation strategy.
- Usually the share of equity in your asset allocation should be 100 minus your age, but you need to have a clear understanding of your risk appetite.
- Different allocations will have varying risk and return levels.
- Regularly rebalance and review your allocation.

Step 10

Understand Asset Classes

In this step, let's try to understand the what, how and why of assets, and how to grow your money intelligently, not emotionally. First things first. What are the types of assets?

Assets	Liquid	Publicly-listed equities	
		Mutual funds	Equity mutual funds
			Debt mutual funds
			Hybrid mutual funds
			Exchange Traded Funds
			Funds of Funds
		Other Equity Investment Vehicles	Portfolio Management Schemes
			Alternative Investment Funds
		Fixed income schemes	Corporate bonds
			Government bonds
			Fixed deposits

	Illiquid	Real estate	
		Alternative investments	Art/Antiques
			Gold
			Private Equity
			Venture Capital
			Hedge funds
			Commodities
		Insurance	

Any asset that has a real-time value and can be converted quickly and easily into cash is a liquid asset. On the other hand, illiquid assets are those assets that cannot be easily converted into cash.

Publicly-listed Equities

Many people consider the stock market to be like a casino. You go in, make some bets, win some, lose some, and get out. Many times, the bets you make are based on the tips you were given at the last get-together by some self-proclaimed stock market guru who made 'a lot' of money on some 'hot' stocks and is now inviting his friends to join the party. You think, 'Oh, what the heck,' and dive in.

That's almost always a bad idea. And this is where most people's distaste for the stock market comes in. They try to game the system, try to trade, then end up losing far more than they bargained for. After this, they swear off the stock market. But this is an emotional response, not a logically reasoned approach.

Indeed there are many tales of people getting ruined in the stock market and losing their life's savings, but what these stories fail to mention is that these people were trading, perhaps buying fundamentally poor quality company stocks, and not holding their investments for a long enough time horizon. This is another finding that may surprise you: Indians are still not making well-informed decisions on the stock market. Studies have shown that emotions tend to affect Indian investors more than data. They mostly buy attention-grabbing stocks. They panic when the market hits a short-term low and rush to sell, booking losses.

Mark Twain wittily said, 'October: This is one of the peculiarly dangerous months to speculate in stocks. The others are July, January, September, April, November, May, March, June, December, August and February.' If you look closely, you will find that all twelve months of the calendar are included in that statement. But the key word that you need to consider is 'speculate'. It's never a good time to speculate but any time could possibly be a good time to invest.

Shares of public companies in India are traded on the main Indian stock exchanges: the Bombay Stock

Exchange, the National Stock Exchange or both. It's surprising to note that equity ownership constitutes only 6% of the Indian household financial wealth, excluding real estate. This is a shockingly low number. Compare this to the US where equity makes up 45% of an individual's portfolio. This is despite the fact that the Bombay Stock Exchange's Sensex has grown over twenty-six times in the last twenty years. This low rate of equity ownership, then, is surely a mistake. Because equity is great for beating inflation over a longer time horizon. Traditionally, stocks offer the highest rate of return if held over a long period of time. At the same time, stocks carry some degree of risk as well.

When you buy publicly-listed equity, you are actually buying a small piece of a company. So when you purchase a share (what I refer to as a 'stock' in this book) in a publicly-listed company, you become one of the co-owners of the company. This is why if the company does well, you prosper. If the company suffers, your stock value goes down too. Since you have a share in the company, you have rights to some part of the company's profits. The company may pass this on to you in the form of dividends or bonus shares, or may reinvest the profits to make your stock value grow further. So far, so good.

So, what accounts for our hesitation? Well, Indians are still very much a security-first people.

By and large, we choose 'safe' investments over 'risky' investments, ignoring the fact that the safe investments (largely fixed deposits) are not only tax inefficient but also the worst hedge against inflation. We Indians also love investing in hard assets like land, real estate and gold (bullion or jewellery), forgetting that such assets can sometimes be quite tough to liquidate.

Frankly, no one (and you can quote me on this) can predict where the market is going. My advice: ignore the headlines. Listen to Paul Samuelson, a Nobel Prize winning economist who said, 'Investing should be more like watching paint dry or watching grass grow. If you want excitement, take $800 and go to Las Vegas.' I like the way Samuelson thinks. To this end, these are the two things you must do.

- Develop a basic understanding of equities as an asset class. What drives returns? Are market valuations cheap or expensive?
- Figure out your time horizon for investing. If your time horizon is long (say eight to ten years), take the plunge. If it is short (two to three years), I would recommend avoiding stocks altogether.

Have you ever read an annual report? Annual reports may seem to be dull documents but if you open one, you will be struck by the fascinating insights inside. They are a great tool to learn more about companies and businesses whose stocks you may want to buy. Most annual reports are easily available online. Good companies do a great job of describing their businesses and performance in detail and don't just throw numbers at you.

The John Maynard Keynes of India

When Diageo, the world's biggest spirits maker, made an open offer to acquire an additional 26% of Vijay Mallya's United Spirits Limited (USL) in 2014, an unassuming professor in Mumbai became richer by 450 crores!

Prof. Shivanand Mankekar owned 1.02% of the company, holding 14.89 lakh shares and was the largest retail investor in USL. Prof. Manekar's lifestyle remains frugal. He lives in a 1,200 square feet, three-bedroom apartment with his wife, son and daughter-in-law in Matunga, and drives a Hyundai Santro. What is amazing is the fact that this almost-anonymous professor is not new to the game. In 2002, he made Rs 100 crores from Pantaloon shares that he had acquired when they were worth Rs 1 crore.

Mankekar taught billionaire banker Uday Kotak at the Jamnalal Bajaj Institute of Management where he continues to teach. Hardly anyone outside the Indian capital markets knows of Mankekar, the only academic among the top twelve private investors in India. Those who know about him, peg his current worth at Rs 1000 crores.

An insider who has been closely following Mankekar's moves says that he believes in a concentrated portfolio with only a few high-performance stocks. He follows a stock's performance and then zeroes in on it, continuously upping his investment. From time to time, he junks the non-performing stocks in his portfolio.

Mutual Funds

A mutual fund is a simple way of investing in a diversified portfolio. Mutual funds pool the money of many investors and construct a portfolio of stocks, bonds and related instruments, chosen by qualified managers. So mutual funds allow you to purchase a collection of stocks, bonds, or other securities that might otherwise be difficult to do on your own. The main advantage of a mutual fund is that it allows you to spread your risk across a diversified basket of investments with only a small amount of money.

Mutual Funds are also regulated, with products being launched by Asset Management Companies only after approvals from the regulators. These steps ensure that small investors' interests are safeguarded.

There are fundamentally five types of mutual funds:
- **Equity mutual funds** that invest in only company stocks.

- **Debt mutual funds** that invest in various kinds of fixed income instruments.
- **Hybrid mutual funds** that invest in a combination of stocks and fixed income instruments.
- **Exchange traded funds** (or ETFs) that mirror the indices like Nifty or Sensex at a low cost.
- **Funds of Funds** can be any combination of the four types above.

Mutual funds have many advantages, which we will discuss shortly, that make them an attractive investment option. However, once again, despite equity mutual funds seeing huge inflows over the past few years, mutual fund penetration in India is dreadfully low. According to a report by Nielsen, in urban India, only 9% of the households invest in mutual funds. A major reason for the low participation is the low level of financial literacy among Indian consumers, which leads to many myths.

I have no patience for baseless myths. Mutual funds have concrete pros and cons and I'd suggest using the points below to make clear-headed investment decisions. Here are the main advantages:

- **Automatic diversification:** If you're just starting out and have a few thousand rupees to invest, it may be almost impossible for you to manage a portfolio that is this highly

diversified. So a mutual fund allows you to easily avoid putting all your eggs in one basket.
- **Professionally managed:** When you buy units in a mutual fund, you have the benefit of having your investment taken care of by experts who have access to specialised research and analysis.
- **Rupee-cost-averaging:** Mutual funds allow investing via a systematic investment plan (or SIP), also known as rupee-cost-averaging. It simply means making regular, scheduled investments instead of buying into the stock market all at once.
- **Transparency:** Mutual funds regularly disclose a lot of information. They are clear about underlying stocks or bonds that are held, expenses and fees, and returns over various time periods.
- **Liquidity:** All mutual funds allow you to buy or sell your fund units every day when the market closes at the fund's Net Asset Value (NAV). This means you can easily sell your funds at any time.

Now let's consider some of the disadvantages:
- **Expense ratio:** Sometimes the fees loaded into a fund can be high. Remember that lower fees directly correlate with higher

performing funds. High-fee funds pay a team of analysts and a fund manager to try to pick the best investments. Because the fund has to pay all of these people, the fees are higher. This would be fine if the returns were also consistently higher, but they may not be. This is why, over time, a low-fee fund that owns an entire range of investments rather than trying to pick and choose 'the best' investments out of their category has higher returns. Before you buy a fund, look at the expense ratio of the fund in the prospectus.
- **False diversification:** Many people own eight to ten different mutual funds and think they are diversified. But when you look inside these mutual funds, all of them own the same stocks or bonds. So you can end up owning a high proportion of a single stock across multiple funds without even knowing it.

What about New Fund Offers? A New Fund Offer (or NFO) is simply a new fund scheme from an asset management company. Think of it like an IPO in the world of mutual funds. Keep in mind that while an established fund can be easily evaluated against its track record, when you invest in a new fund, you're wading into unchartered waters. I suggest finding out who the fund manager is. If the fund manager has a great track record, you're off to a good start.

Please also disregard the myth of a low Net Asset Value (NAV). You may have heard this often: Fund A with an NAV of 10 is cheap compared to Fund B with an NAV of 100. Nothing could be farther from the truth. Remember that a low or high NAV number has no bearing on the performance of the fund whatsoever. Instead, look at the pace of appreciation of the NAV over time.

Other equity investment vehicles

Besides mutual funds, equity investments can made through a variety of other investment vehicles. These are commonly used by more experienced investors. Let me briefly touch upon two of them:
- **Portfolio Management Schemes** (PMS): PMS are direct equity portfolios that are run by various portfolio managers. Unlike a mutual fund, PMS strategies can be customised for each individual investor. Given that PMS require a slightly higher degree of investor experience and understanding, regulators have prescribed minimum investment criteria for these products. PMS are generally favoured by high net worth investors.

- **Alternate Investment Funds** (AIF): AIF are a recent entrant into the Indian markets. These are again specialised portfolios run by portfolio managers, with the objective of capturing the crests and troughs of the market. They are therefore free to use derivatives as well. AIFs, too, require a deep knowledge and long experience of investing, and are considered by institutions and high net worth individuals.

So, direct stocks vs. mutual funds, which way should you go? Direct equity and equity mutual funds come with their own pluses and minuses. How does one choose between the two? Consider these points:

- Mutual funds are a good option for someone starting out. Mutual funds are a good way to gain experience. It takes less effort, less time, less experience and less specialised knowledge to get good returns from equity mutual funds than it does from directly investing in stocks.
- Equities are complex as they come in a bewildering array of sectors, industries, sizes, financial structures, promoter track records, competitive scenarios and more. When you invest in a fund from a good fund house, there is a full-fledged research department to keep tabs on all of this.

- If you're interested in following a specific company's growth, consider investing directly in stocks. Unlike funds, stocks are no-fee. Also, you will get tax-free dividends and capital gains over one year.
- History shows that investing in a large cap blue chip company at a fair price has rarely ever gone wrong in the long run. If you have an appetite for risk, you could also invest in small-cap or mid-cap stocks that are likely to become tomorrow's large-cap blue chips.
- Stocks promise higher returns. As you take more risk and subject your portfolio to more volatility, the potential for higher returns also increases. But again, you should attempt this only if you are personally passionate about stocks or have a good investment advisor.

To summarise, if you're a first-time investor in equities, begin with mutual funds. As you learn and gain experience, you can start building a long-term direct stock portfolio.

Fixed Income Schemes

What is fixed income? Rather simple. Fixed income is income earned from an investment at a standard (or more or less predictable) rate of return. Corporate and government bonds are examples of fixed income investments and so is a fixed deposit.

So what exactly is a bond? The best way to understand a bond is to think of it like a loan. When you invest in bonds, you are lending money to the government or a company. In return for this loan, the bond issuer will pay you interest for the term of the loan. Bonds provide mostly regular, stable returns because you know how much money you will get back at the end of your term. On maturity, you also get your principal amount back.

India has a high fixed income penetration because security is the top concern for Indian investors. They are easily lured to investments that promise returns that are regular, even if low. It's this approach that makes Indian investors mostly prefer avenues like fixed deposits, EPF, PPF, IVP, NSS, NSC along with LIC policies (the most preferred investment avenue). One of the early Secretaries of the US Treasury, Andrew Mellon, joked, 'Gentlemen prefer bonds!' It certainly seems to hold good for Indians.

However, during the last few years bank interest rates have been dropping, staying generally below the inflation rate. In this situation, is it wise to deposit large portions of your money in banks as fixed deposits? Do we have the whole picture of fixed income? What sort of returns do fixed income assets give you?

Fixed Income Type	Average Yield	Term	Benchmark Portfolio
Corporate Bonds, ICDs, FD, Arbitrage	8.21%	2000–15	NSE Bond Index: Composite
Government Bonds	8.22%	2000–15	NSE Bond Index: Dated Govt. Securities
CD, CP, Liquid	6.99%	2000–15	NSE Bond Index: Treasury Bill
Short Term MF	8.47%	2000–15	NSE Bond Index: Short Term
Long Term MF	8.25%	2000–15	NSE Bond Index: Long Term
Mid Term MF	7.97%	2000–15	NSE Bond Index: Medium Term
Fixed Maturity Plan (FMPs)	Depends on interest rate cycle	2000–15	

From the table, you would realize that fixed income assets cannot help you beat inflation or truly grow your wealth. So why do Indians love fixed income assets? Because they tend to believe in many myths about it. These are:

- **Everything stays 'fixed' in fixed income:** The word 'fixed' can be a misnomer. Did you know that if interest rates fall, bond prices rise and if interest rates increase then bond prices fall?

If you weren't aware of this and liquidated your investments during a rising interest rate cycle, your bond valuations would have taken a hit.
- **Tax-free bonds offer compounded returns:** It's a common misconception that tax-free bonds offer compounded interest. In fact, most tax-free bonds offer coupons or interest that are paid out annually, and then the investor is responsible for re-investing the coupon.
- **Fixed deposits are risk-free:** A fixed deposit is a loan you have extended to the bank. If the bank defaults, creditors can stand to lose their money. The government of India guarantees the return of up to one lakh of the depositor's money with scheduled commercial banks. Cooperative banks are not a part of this undertaking.

So, every investor experiences a dilemma. 'If I invest in equity, I will lose money in case the market goes down but if I don't invest in equity, I will miss out from gains in case the market rises.' How is an investor to balance this conflict? By being realistic. We know that no investments are without risk. If you seek to gain from an investment, you have to allow the possibility of loss. Frankly, a goal of avoiding losses at all counts will only lead to poor returns. I'd say that the right approach is diversification. Balance the hits and flops.

Despite the comparatively lower rates of return, there are certain areas where fixed income emerges as the clear winner over equity.

- **Low risk of default:** Any loan comes with a risk of default. However, in government securities or sovereign debt, the risk of default can be assumed to be much lower than the default risk associated with private sector debt. Corporate bonds typically carry more risk. However, in the event of a company being placed into liquidation, bonds holders rank high amongst the creditors and are paid out before the equity shareholders.
- **Low market risk:** Bonds differ from equities in an important aspect. In order to realise your profit (or loss) on an equity, you must sell the instrument back to the market at whatever price the market happens to be quoting. But with the vast majority of bonds, the redemption date and amount are fixed in advance, thereby reducing your reliance on fickle market sentiment or changing liquidity. This is a vital advantage for people who have cash to invest now but who know that they will want to spend it at some point in the future.

Now let us turn our attention to illiquid assets.

Although I'm writing a book about wealth, when faced with deep, complicated concepts, I look to history. Imagine a man from one of the medieval Indian kingdoms of 1000 AD, time travelling to the present day and finding this book on my desk. The chap would be confounded at the strange and intricate ways humans have devised to earn money in the twenty-first century. What would he make of mutual funds, I wonder. Or of life insurance, private equity and hedge funds?

But we must not underestimate the past. The instruments of investment may have become multidimensional but the basic instinct of accumulating wealth on an investment has been a part of human consciousness for millennia. Did you know, for instance, that Jain merchants and portfolio capitalists proliferated during Mughal rule? And much before that, the *Arthashastra*, Chanakya's seminal book about economic policy, spoke of the necessity of wealth and the many ways of acquiring it. I speak of history because although our ancestors would have found the intricacies of the modern day financial markets to be alien concepts, they were well aware of our present topic of discussion: illiquid assets.

Some examples of illiquid assets include real estate, antiques, jewellery and collectibles such as art, coins and stamps. For the more exotic, there are even vintage cars, wine, rare whiskey and so on. Even though they cannot be readily transformed into money, people have always known the value of collecting such assets. The advantages of illiquid assets are many. People who are willing to retain them for a long time horizon know that the asset can be sold for many times its original value.

Of course, the main disadvantage of illiquid assets lies in their name itself. They are no good when you need money immediately. Illiquid assets are not amenable to liquidity. In fact, desperate people have been known to sell valuable illiquid assets at deep, loss-making discounts.

Real estate

The Mahabharata war started when Duryodhana famously said that he would not be willing to part with even a speck of land that was the size of a needle point to the Pandavas. Rock inscriptions from thousands of years ago and written in Pali and Sanskrit have been found all over India. They speak, in painstaking detail, about the sizable tracts of land bestowed upon lucky gentlemen by the king. The *Tuzuk-e-Jahangiri*, Mughal emperor Jahangir's autobiography, is filled with records of land gifted to the highest benefactors. So many Partition stories from 1947 are about land estates left behind in a country no longer their own. And closer still, movies from the '80s about greedy landowners were super hits in India, complete with Bappi Lahiri music and angry young men. The point I'm trying to make here is that the concept of land as wealth is embedded in our country's consciousness. It's the most aspirational aspect of *roti-kapda-makaan*.

Real estate is something tangible that you can touch. Its tangible nature makes it seem more real, and hence secure, to us. But the reality is that a home does not make a good investment if you're planning to live in it. Just like you may never sell that beautiful pair of gold *jhumkis* or necklace your grandmother passed on to you, your home is essentially for your own consumption.

So, should you rent or buy? 'Is that even a question?' you must be thinking. Buying a house is so inherently a part of our plans of making it big that we never even stop to consider why.

If a house that I live in is not an asset, why should I buy it? Why can't I rent instead? The assertion may seem revolutionary, but there is a vocal minority of financial experts who hold that it does not make sense to buy a house to live in. While I have known this for a while, it was only recently that I discovered that this is quite a controversial concept.

I like to take a simple view of things. Let's assume you can rent a property for Rs 50,000 per month.

What if I told you that you have the option to buy the same property, and with your current financial situation, you will be able to ensure that the EMI per month on your home loan will be Rs 50,000 per month as well?

Now, there is no right or wrong answer to buying vs. renting. It is, as with most situations about money, subjective. Here are my thoughts:

In case you do not require a loan to purchase real estate, by all means go ahead. But remember, all the principles we have discussed so far apply. Make sure you are buying an asset at the right price.

In case you need to take a loan to fund your purchase, here are some additional pointers. If you are able to find an asset where your EMI on the loan is roughly the same as the rent that you will pay, it is likely to be worth it to buy and not rent. In case the rent is much lower than the potential EMI, then it may be better for you to postpone your purchase till there is a closer parity between the EMI and rent. This is where most potential Indian homebuyers find themselves today. With the rapid pace of price appreciation in the last decade, real asset prices are so high that in most large Indian cities, it is better to stay on rent than purchase an apartment.

Deciding between buying and renting a house depends on two factors: One, capital appreciation, which is another way of saying how much your property grows in value. Two, rental yield, which is the percentage of the house price you pay in rent every year.

$$\text{Rental Yield} = \frac{\text{Annual Rent}}{\text{Cost of the property}}$$

Let's take two individuals, Sulekha and Saurabh. Both have an investible surplus of Rs 1 crore today. Sulekha rents a two-bedroom apartment in Vile Parle, Mumbai, for Rs 45,000 per month, with her rent rising at 5% every year. Saurabh, on the other hand, buys an identical apartment next door to that of Sulekha for a list price of Rs 1.5 crores.

If Saurabh makes a down payment of Rs 1 crore, and takes a loan for the balance, he is now required to pay an EMI of roughly Rs 50,000 per month (assuming he has borrowed Rs 50 lakhs at 10% per year for twenty years). The situation after twenty years would look something like this:

Sulekha invested her surplus Rs 1 crore at 9% per year, and paid rent out of the capital she saved. At the end of the twenty year period, her total savings are 1.22 crores. Saurabh now owns the apartment completely, having paid off the entire home loan. Assuming a 3% annual appreciation in his property, his asset is now worth Rs 2.7 crores. In this situation, clearly it was better to buy than rent. But what if Sulekha had been able to get better returns on her investments? Now refer to the table below.

Return per year on ₹ Cr	Value of investment after 20 years
9% per year	₹ 1.22 Crs
10% per year	₹ 1.92 Crs
11% per year	₹ 2.79 Crs
12% per year	₹ 3.88 Crs

As you can see, the rate of return makes all the difference. Instead of investing in a 9% fixed deposit, if Sulekha had invested in a mixed portfolio of equities and bonds, earning 12% per year, she would have ended up much better off than Saurabh. So before you go and make this large investment of buying real estate based on 'accepted wisdom' and clichés, take a look at the numbers. Remember, they never lie.

Buying real estate is a huge financial and emotional investment. It is probably one of the biggest and most complicated things you will ever do. It makes sense to deeply understand everything related to it before you take the plunge. Obviously I cannot go into each and every detail here, but I hope to point you in the right direction.

Here come a couple of rather controversial assertions. Traditionally, buying a house has been the safe, secure thing to do, while equity is supposed to be for the risk takers. But why? Let's put some pressure on these myths and shake up the numbers to see if they add up. It's time to examine these myths:

- **Real estate gives better returns than equity:** Let's see which is a better investment option, stocks or real estate. If you invested in real estate between 2007 and 2014, there was an even better investment option: buying shares of India's largest housing finance company, Housing Development Finance Corporation (HDFC). If you bought a house, you would have had to choose the location carefully. 89 of the 195 location pockets across 25 cities tracked by the National Housing Bank (NHB) returned less than a bank fixed deposit. In fact, the BSE Realty Index lost nearly 80% of its value during this period. By comparison, the share price of HDFC went up more than three-times during this period.

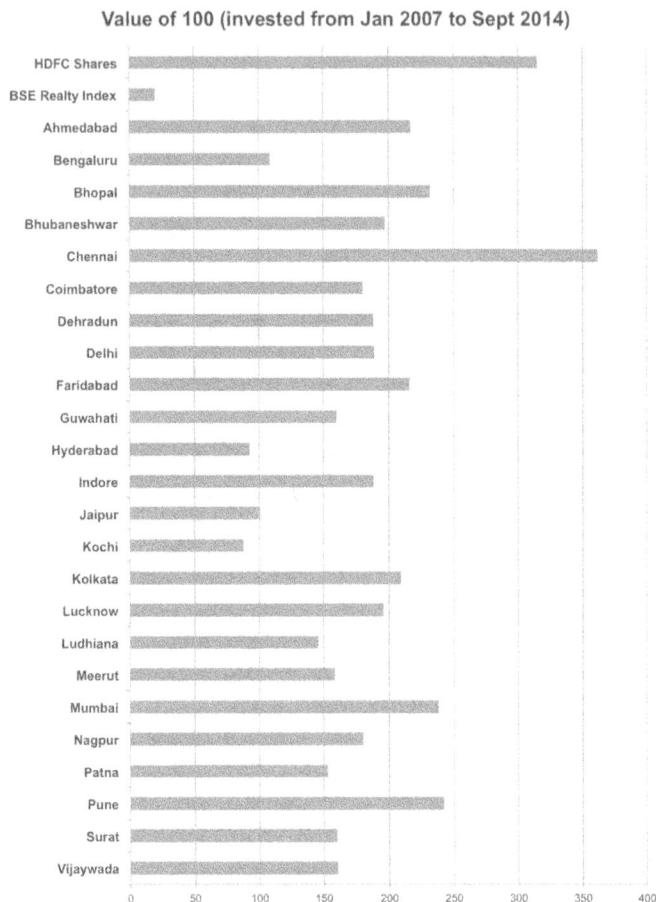

Value of 100 (invested from Jan 2007 to Sept 2014)

Source: Livemint.com

- **Real estate is a safer investment option than equity:** For most people, risk comes entwined with the stock market while real estate seems to be a solid, safe option. Let's run some numbers and verify this psychology. Below, we have the data for Mumbai's best-real-estate-performance locality of Colaba. The average ten-year return was 8.07% with the lowest being 2.09% (1996–2006) and the highest being 14.37% (2003–2013). Volatile? Absolutely! The returns are even more unstable if you take a shorter time period of five or eight years. If you look at a comparative return on the Nifty, it is far superior with much lesser volatility. Not a single ten-year return is negative in this case. So which is the better investment option? You have all the information to make the decision.

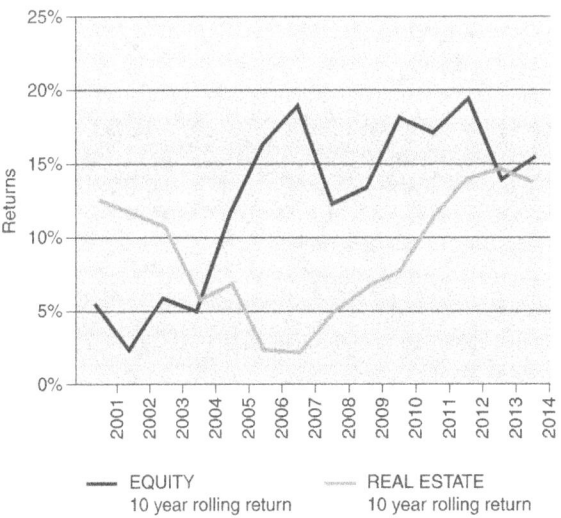

Source: Government ready reckoner and bseindia.com

Robert Shiller, the Nobel Prize-winning economist, once suggested, 'It would perhaps be smarter, if wealth accumulation is your goal, to rent and put money in the stock market, which has historically shown much higher returns than the housing market.'

Thus, real estate can be quite volatile. However, unlike equities, real estate prices are not tracked on a daily basis and hence a drop does not cause widespread panic selling, like it does with equity. Similarly when prices rise, investors do not sell to book profits in a hurry. Given its nature, real estate is usually held for long periods and hence allows the power of compounding to truly play out. It is easy to get carried away by stories of people who bought property in the 1950's for literally a few thousands and sold it recently for crores. But if you do the math, you will find that the overall compounded growth was not more than 10% per year. The return after tax may fall even below this. It's a good return, but it's not astounding.

One more thing: Mark Twain famously said, 'Buy land, they're not making it anymore.' When you own a residential flat or commercial property in a building, what you are buying is fractional ownership of the underlying land on which the building stands. So when FSI norms change in your favour, ideally you should be able to profit from it. But it will be hard unless all of the building society members come together to agree to do something about this. Most people that have profited handsomely from real estate have done it on the back of land ownership, not fractional ownership.

I know young people who start getting anxious just after beginning their first jobs. They want to buy a house because that's the way it goes. But think about it, have they paid off their student loans? Have they started investing? Are they saving for retirement? Do they even have the budget to buy a house? These are important questions they must ask themselves before committing to this enormous investment, which may or may not be a sound one.

Alternative investments

Again and again I keep bringing us back to a diversified portfolio. In that sense, once you have stocks, fixed income and property in your asset allocation, you may think that you're all done. And you probably are. But not before you consider the newest set of investment options: alternative investments.

To keep it simple, an alternative is any investment that is not a stock, a bond, cash or real estate. Alternative investments include a range of assets from art, gold and commodities to derivatives and partnerships in private businesses. Think venture capital, private equity, hedge funds, Real Estate

Investment Trusts (REITs), commodities as well as real assets such as precious metals, rare coins, wine, art and more.

Now, usually these seem to be the arena of suited-booted, fast talking High Net Worth Individuals (or HNIs), going in and out of five-star hotels and knowing exactly what they are doing with their money. It all seems glamorous and intimidating. But I'm here to demystify the alternatives for you.

Why alternatives, you may ask. Because many of them are not directly correlated with the stock market. They are driven by the knowledge that a portfolio of traditional equities and fixed income has risk and return limitations. Alternatives promise good uncorrelated returns when held for a long time horizon. Jonathan Clements of the Wall Street Journal says that alternatives are the financial world's 'Holy Grail...an investment that will generate decent long-run returns and post gains when stocks are suffering.' This is great for portfolio protection. So let's examine some alternative investments.

It has been joked that the golden rule is that those who have the gold make the rules. And boy, aren't we Indians obsessed with gold? Our country has a long history, going back thousands of years, of buying gold because it has been entwined with religious and cultural beliefs. Over the centuries, Indian households have piled up as much as 20,470 tonnes of gold until March 2013, worth 60.61 lakh crore, a historic high. Coupled with the 5,000 tonnes of gold held by Indian temples and 558 tonnes of the Central Bank's holdings, gold stocks at known sources in India (the world's largest consumer) represent more than 75% of its GDP.

While gold is an accepted form of alternative investments, is it an advisable one? Only when held in a practical, tradable form such as coins or bars, also known as bullion. Like your house, you're not going to sell your jewellery unless you're in dire straits. And trust me, you will not be trading it for profit then. So please don't think of gold jewellery as an investment. It's simply for your pleasure. That said, investors can now invest in gold through Gold Exchange-Traded Funds (or ETFs) for as low as 500 rupees per month. This offers anyone the chance to own the yellow metal without having to come up with high lump sums or deal with the hassles of physical storage.

Another 'hot' alternative investment category is Private Equity (or PE). Private equity is exactly what it sounds like. The opposite of public equity, PE is simply equity capital that is not quoted on a public exchange such as the BSE or NSE. Private equity firms typically raise funds from non-institutional and institutional investors. The funds are used to place investments in promising private companies.

The traditional view of start-ups (fuelled by stories of Steve Jobs or Bill Gates) is that they begin in garages somewhere in Silicon Valley, California. Frankly, nowadays there are solid structures dedicated to help start-ups grow and thrive. Venture capital is a subset of private equity that specialises in investing in early-stage to growth-stage companies. It's a risky asset class, but has been known to provide humongous returns when a successful liquidity event happens. Think of venture capitalists who took their chances on Google or Facebook.

Another alternative investment is the hedge fund. Think of a hedge fund as a partnership of investors. Hedge funds are pooled investment funds which use bold, high-risk strategies to generate big windfalls.

Finally, of course, are 'real' assets. These are physical assets that have fundamental value. Think precious metal as well as luxury and collectible goods like fine wines, art, jewellery, rare coins, stamps, vintage cars and so on. You can buy these directly or invest with a fund, such as an art fund.

But remember what Peter Lynch once said. 'Invest in what you know.' While he was talking of stocks, the concept applies to any and all investments. Since alternative investments are so varied, they require a high degree of expertise on the investor's part. Watch out for these classic risks:

- **Difficult to value:** Determining the current market value can be a bit of a chore for alternatives like real assets.

- **Low liquidity:** Alternatives such as art or coins can be difficult to sell. You may have to wait a long time until you find buyers or get the price you have in mind.
- **Costly trading:** Handling, storing and selling of alternatives can involve high fees and commissions.
- **Market correlation:** During volatile periods, some investors find that alternatives may have a high correlation to the market, which they did not anticipate.
- **Opaque returns:** It may become difficult for a first-time alternatives investor to see all the hidden risks.
- **High fees:** Alternative investment options come with high embedded fees, typically a 2% per year management charge plus a 20% profit share.

Insurance

Let me start by saying that insurance is a part of any sound financial plan. Since we have been looking over our shoulder at ancient history in this step, you will be surprised to know that insurance is as old as Indian trade. When merchants from Gujarat and Tamil Nadu travelled across the seas two thousand years ago, they insured themselves with marine contracts. This was a smart move and we would do well to learn from it.

Insurance protects us from all kinds of financial risk. Life insurance helps us secure our loved ones in case of our death. Health insurance allows us to get proper medical aid without worrying about the costs. Car insurance protects us from bankruptcy in the unfortunate event of a collision. A good insurance policy is priceless when it comes to protecting against risk.

In addition, insurance is a great tax-saving instrument for investment. There are products like Unit Linked Insurance Plans (ULIPs) and Endowment Plans, which promise to increase your money by a higher rate than a traditional insurance plan would.

Term insurance is straightforward. You pay a premium throughout your life. After your death, your beneficiaries are rewarded with a large sum of money, known as the death benefit. The premium is quite low compared to the relatively large benefits.

For example, let's consider a thirty-five-year-old woman. She pays Rs 5,500 per year for a thirty-year term policy for a cover of Rs 25 lakhs. In effect, she pays a total of Rs 1.65 lakhs till the age of 65 in return for a tax-free sum of 25 lakhs insured to her beneficiary. By contrast, if she were to merely invest the same Rs 5,500 and earn an annually compounded return of 12%, she would only get an assured return of Rs 14.86 lakhs (before tax) after thirty years. In effect, a term life insurance provides a high rate of return for your beneficiaries. I consider it a low price for a high degree of peace of mind that my family will be taken care of after me.

There are some kinds of insurance that work as investments too. In these cases, besides the death benefit, the policyholder receives an assured sum before his or her death, when the policy expires. As is expected, you pay a much higher premium for these. There are some benefits of insurance as investment. The returns are tax-free. It can be used as collateral against loans. And they provide additional benefits in case of critical illness.

But examine a little closely and you will find that two out of these three benefits can be easily gained from other asset classes, at lower costs and probably higher returns. Using permanent life insurance as an investment may make sense for high net worth individuals looking to minimise taxation. But if you want to invest for a long time-horizon, I would suggest buying term and investing the difference in the markets. What does this mean? It comes from the idea that term insurance is the cheapest type of insurance for most people. This leaves them with money to invest in other instruments like equity or fixed income, based on their appetite.

People tend to allocate 5% to 10% of their overall asset allocation to alternative investment options.

Also, given that there are minimum ticket sizes to enter most alternative investment options, many Indians give them a miss. I would say that you should consider entering this asset class only once you are fully invested in the liquid asset classes.

Key Takeaways

- Assets can be liquid or illiquid. Liquid assets are those that can be converted relatively quickly into cash. Those that can't are called illiquid assets.
- Common types of liquid assets include publicly listed equities, mutual funds, fixed income schemes and other investment vehicles.
- Mutual funds are an excellent way of investing for those who may not have professional expertise in the underlying market.
- While fixed income products are relatively safer than equity-linked products they come with their fair share of risks.
- Common illiquid assets include real estate, alternative investments and insurance.
- Illiquid assets can sometimes be used as a hedge against one's liquid investments.
- Consider carefully the question of whether to own or rent your own home. The decision will depend on several financial variables.

- Alternative investments should only be considered if you have in-depth knowledge. Keep in mind that these are difficult to liquidate in moments of crisis.
- Insurance is worth considering but first evaluate whether the premium is justified.

Step 11

Knowledge, focus, patience, review

Now that you have understood the importance of asset allocation and gained an understanding of asset classes, what are the qualities that will enable you to navigate the world of wealth building? Here are a few recommendations:
- Educate yourself as a continuous process
- Cut out the noise and focus on your plan
- Appreciate the value of time and patience
- Constantly track and review

Educate yourself as a continuous process

An investment advisor once joked that there are primarily three different types of investors:
- Those who don't know anything. They account for 10%.
- Those who know a little. They're around 10%.

- Those who don't know that they don't know anything. They are about 80%.

I reiterate that you should invest in things that you absolutely believe in and fully understand. I like investing in direct stocks and mutual funds that add value to my portfolio and fixed income schemes that don't take undue risk. These investments come with specific objectives that I'm looking for and are rock solid. In such cases I am hardly bothered when prices fall in the short term. In fact, I feel motivated to buy more when prices fall because of my conviction in the company I bought. So why shouldn't I acquire more of a good thing at an attractive price?

But how would you go about understanding an investment opportunity unless you are willing to study it? If I wanted to spoon-feed you, instead of writing this book I would have just made an investment plan for you and let you roll with it. That would be the easy way. Or would it? What I have learned with my experience is that there is no easy way. Nor do investments come with a ready template. You are unique, so are your needs, and therefore your investments will also have to be exclusive to you.

Knowledge is power and power is wealth. I thrive on making my own decisions after understanding a problem and all its intricacies. And so far, this approach has worked for me. This is why instead of handing you a ready plan, I'm offering you this book as a diving board. I'm not saying that this book is the final word on investing. But it is certainly a starting point to make you more aware, make you ask the right questions and avoid the most common mistakes.

Here are some ways in which you can build your own personal knowledge in such matters:

- Always read the fine print of every document and prospectus. Ensure that you absorb all the implications and risks of your investment.
- Visit online resources that contain a wealth of information. A list of resources is provided at the end of this book.
- Meet with other investors. When investing in mutual funds, try meeting fund managers. Such meetings can be valuable learning opportunities.
- Build a reading list of books that you ought to read and take out time to peruse them. Several books are listed at the end of this book and they can be excellent starting points that will open your mind to additional reading.

Cut out the noise and focus

There is too much noise in our world. A newsflash from the television or the Internet suggests that trends are constantly shifting, moving and fluctuating. Information changes in a heartbeat. Blink and you miss it.

This is the information age. The problem is that there is so much information in our world that one doesn't know what to absorb, whom to trust and where to look. Between the cacophony of screaming newspaper headlines, the constantly moving tickers at the bottom of the television screen and the barrage of updates from Facebook, Twitter, WhatsApp and Snapchat, where is the *real* information?

Whether it's a discussion about the fiscal deficit or political uncertainty, it's easy to get lost in the noise and make ill-informed decisions. As investors trying to make safe returns on our investments or cutting losses, how do we chart the waters of this flood of information?

In the 1980s, with government-controlled television and radio, information was tightly regulated and hard to come by. With the opening of the markets, the '90s saw the cable boom and a new era of private news channels dawned. Suddenly, we were connected to all the corners of the world. The hidden parts of our country as well as of our financial markets were ours to pore over while sitting in our living rooms watching TV.

The twenty-first century changed all of this. Not only did the competition in the TRP ratings fuel the twenty-four-hour news cycle but it also unleashed upon us the barrage of talking heads on TV that never seem to shut up. According to them, one day India was shining and a few months later we were on the brink of doom. Add to this a life-changing phenomenon: the arrival of the Internet.

Until the early '90s, communication also remained limited because of the constraints of size and costs. Radio and television were curtailed by the costs of airtime, print media by the costs of space. But the Internet broke all these barriers. Anyone with an Internet connection is now a pundit, a guru or an expert (on pretty much everything under the sun). Data, data, data is the clarion call of this age.

New times call for new strategies. One must exercise restraint in this era. Although it's hard to get to the bottom-line, we can try separating the grain from the chaff with some simple rules.

First, don't believe everything you hear. Seriously, use your common sense. If you start believing every Tom, Dick and Harry as also the multiple WhatsApp forwards, Facebook updates, Twitter headlines and inflammatory blogs, you will be the first victim of panic and will end up doing something stupid.

Second, always authenticate information. Don't start a stampede when you hear something. Validate the source. 'Who is saying it?' is the first question to ask. Determine where the news is coming from, why they are saying it, and what's in it for them. Only trust the source that has a track record of providing authentic information.

The Monkey Man

Once upon a time a stranger arrived in a village and told the residents that he would be willing to buy monkeys from them for Rs 10 each. Familiar with the surrounding jungles, the villagers knew that there were many monkeys that could be easily caught in the forest. The stranger bought two thousand monkeys over the next few days.

As the availability of monkeys began declining, the villagers began returning to their agricultural duties. The stranger upped his offer to Rs 20 per monkey. The excited villagers doubled their efforts and caught yet another thousand monkeys.

Monkeys now became a rarity. It was becoming impossible to find any. The villagers were about to give up when the stranger announced that he was now willing to offer Rs 40. The tired villagers excitedly devised new ways to source monkeys and managed to catch five hundred more.

The stranger then announced that owing to the scarcity of monkeys in the forest, he would now be willing to buy the animals for Rs 100 each. In the same breath, he told the villagers that he was going to the city on some important business but his assistant would act on his behalf.

The assistant shrewdly told the villagers, 'My boss is mad. He has 3500 monkeys in that massive cage and yet wants to buy more. Why don't you chaps buy the monkeys from me at Rs 50 each and when my boss comes back you can sell those animals back to him for Rs 100.'

There was a mad rush to buy the animals as the villagers dipped into their life savings to corner the monkey supply. Soon the massive cage was empty. The villagers had been paid Rs 60,000 to catch those monkeys and they had parted with Rs 1,75,000 to buy them back!

Is it necessary to mention that neither the stranger nor his assistant were ever seen in the village again? It probably explains the origins of the term 'monkey business'!

The downside of the information avalanche is that it buries the most important aspect of financial planning: your portfolio or asset allocation. This is something we have discussed at length previously in this book. I cannot stress enough the importance of a well-balanced portfolio. It could be the difference between consistent returns and disappointing ones.

Your portfolio is your plan and you must follow it. It is the anchor that gives stability in the flood of information. Hold on, stick with it, and you will navigate successfully. Think of it as your Pole Star. When the waters of information arbitrage threaten to drown you, trust the only constant you have: your asset allocation.

Appreciate the value of time and patience

As we saw when we discussed the wealth trinity of risk, return and time, the last factor is critical. One needs to have a long enough time-horizon to judge performance and allow at least three to five years for the market cycles to play out. There is the proverb that says 'Time heals all wounds'. It applies perfectly to the world of investing. Short term booms and busts get averaged out over a longer time horizon.

The 641 crore windfall
Mohammed Anwar Ahmed lived in the small town of Amalner in district Jalgaon, Maharashtra. His father owned a large plot of farmland and, after his death in 1980, his four sons sold the land and divided the sale proceeds of Rs 80,000 equally among themselves. Mohammed, the youngest of the four brothers was twenty-seven at the time. He was confused about the direction that he should take. Amalner's only significant business was a factory set up by Azim Premji's father to manufacturer vegetable ghee, vanaspati and refined oils. It was called Western India Vegetable Products Ltd.

One day while Mohammed was sipping tea at a stall in Amalner, a stockbroker from Mumbai stopped by to make enquiries. The broker had come to Amalner to buy as many shares that he could find for some Mumbai-based clients. 'Do you know people who own shares in that factory?' he asked Mohammed as he gestured towards the vanaspati plant. Mohammed replied that the owners lived in Mumbai but he ended up spending fifteen minutes with the broker in the process. During those fifteen minutes he received the education of a lifetime. He learnt that owning a share could make him a part-owner in the company.

Mohammed helped the broker visit neighbours and collect shares from willing sellers. Mohammed also acquired a hundred shares of Rs 100 face value, thus investing half of the Rs 20,000 that he had received as his share of the land sale proceeds. He started a trading business with the remaining money. From that day onwards, Mohammed began thinking of himself as part-owner of the company and firmly decided that he would not sell his shares for as long as Azim Premji remained at the helm. Here's what happened.

- *1980: 100 shares were bought at Rs 100 face value for Rs 10,000 in total.*
- *1981: 1:1 bonus was declared. He now had 200 shares.*
- *1985: Another 1:1 bonus was announced. He now had 400 shares.*
- *1986: Shares were split to Rs 10. He now had 4000 shares.*
- *1987: Announcement of 1:1 bonus. He now had 8000 shares.*

1989: Another 1:1 bonus. Now he had 16,000 shares.
1992: Yet another 1:1 bonus. His holding was now 32,000 shares.
1995: Announcement of another 1:1 bonus. His shares doubled to 64,000.
1997: Mega 2:1 bonus announced. He now held 1,92,000 shares.
1999: Rs 10 Shares were split to Rs 2. He now had 9,60,000 shares.
2004: Another 2:1 bonus was declared. He thus had 28,80,000 shares.
2005: A 1:1 bonus was announced. He now held 57,60,000 shares.
2010: A 2:3 bonus was announced. He now had 96,00,000 shares.

The current market price is over Rs 545 per share. His holding is worth Rs 523 crores. This is not including the dividends that the company paid out every year. He cumulatively received Rs 118 crores as dividend. By investing Rs 10,000 and waiting patiently over an extended period of time Mohammed gained 641 crores!

Constantly track and review

OK, so you have understood the basics of a good investment plan and created a well-balanced portfolio for yourself. But if you do not track and maintain it, you are throwing all the benefits to the wind. Diversified asset allocation, tracking and rebalancing are the three friends you should never let go of.

You can't control what you can't measure. Like I have been telling you throughout the book: I'm a numbers guy. Their solidity is the foundation on which I build all my decisions, and not on speculative theories. So believe me when I tell you this: if you cannot measure it, you cannot control it.

We have discussed the basis of successfully growing your wealth through the chapters of this book. But even if you implement absolutely everything to the last detail, without regularly tracking and monitoring the key parameters of your asset allocation plan, your portfolio is sure to underperform. Because if you don't track, you lose critical oversight.

So how do you measure and control things easily and smartly? Simply by seeing your entire financial life, with all the associated parameters, in one view. If you see your portfolio clearly and transparently, you will immediately spot any deviations from the expected results. It's then easy to identify unnatural behaviour and take actions to protect yourself from impending financial disasters.

The Information-Enabled Farmer
Reuters Market Light (or RML), is a subsidiary of Thomson Reuters India that supplies farm report data

to mobile phones. This service provides individual farmers with 'customised, localised and personalised' weather forecasts, local crop prices, agricultural news and crop advisory information, in the form of SMS messages sent to their mobile phones in their local language. The founder of RML, Amit Mehra, saw an opportunity in rural India where he recognised a problem farmers were facing: the lack of accurate data that could potentially affect their yield, income and livelihood. He decided to empower the farmers with information pertaining to their daily farming needs.

RML has managed to help farmers disperse their market risks, by deciding when and where to sell their produce to maximise profits. There has been a 5.2% reduction in price dispersion across markets due to the availability of the service. The company estimates that farmers have reaped significant returns on their investment, achieving up to Rs 2,00,000 of additional profits, and savings of nearly Rs 4,00,000 by using RML alerts. What's more is that 90% of the farmers believed they benefited from the RML service and over 80% were willing to pay for it.

So how does one track one's portfolio successfully and without confusion? As your portfolio grows, so does the danger of developing liabilities and blind spots. It's easy to get lost in a world of information overload. I know because five years ago I faced the same problem.

The next time you find the world of wealth management confusing, remember that wealth is not complex and its management should not be either. There are many investment managers who hide or disguise information in order to sell their own investments to you. Do not blindly depend on your financial advisor. Do your own homework. Track everything. The person who doesn't know where his next rupee is coming from usually doesn't know where his last rupee went.

The demystification of wealth management with the help of technology has already begun. There are now tools available that let users compare rates and features of various investment options, offer automated advice and help with retirement goals and planning. The greatest value of digitisation is in investment tracking and management where you can without any hassles improve workflow and minimise manual operations to make your investment life simple and easy.

So here are my two bits: let your money control you and you will be forever stressed and strung out. Bring your finances under your control and you will laugh all the way to the bank.

Key Takeaways

- Educate yourself as a continuous process. Read the fine print of offer documents. Read relevant books.

- Cut out the noise and follow your plan. Do not get swayed by market sentiments.
- There is no substitute for time in garnering returns.
- Constantly track and review your portfolio.

Step 12

Leverage good debt

I remember how in the 1970's, India was still a sluggish elephant. The economy was controlled by the government. A home loan was difficult to come by. People generally didn't indulge in shopping sprees because frankly, there wasn't much to shop for.

The 80's saw the first signs of Indian consumerism. The Maruti 800 appeared on Indian roads. Colour television—introduced just before the Asian Games held in New Delhi in 1982—heralded an era of the 'foreign' experience for millions of Indians right here at home.

But when the markets really opened in the '90s, it was like a well of desire had been tapped into in the country. Everywhere you looked there were things to buy and people to buy them. India turned from a country of savers into a country of consumers. And to capitalise on this change came the easily available credit cards pushed by banks on to people who had, historically, no experience of dealing with credit.

Until then, we were suspicious about owing debt. But now, with 'Buy on EMI' schemes and easy payment options, we find it hard to resist the barrage of consumer goods flooding the markets. By the time the recession of 2008 rolled around, this frenzy had claimed many victims. A comedian summed up the situation well : there are three kinds of people these days—the haves, the have-nots, and the have-not-paid-for-what-they-haves.

Debt is a four-letter word

These days there are people who twist and turn in their beds all night, hiding the state of their finances from their spouse and children, unable to sleep because they have racked up credit card debts of lakhs of rupees.

According to industry reports, the amount of outstanding credit card debt in India tripled between 2004 and 2007. Today, it's a mark of people's economic troubles that there are services such as the SBI's financial counselling centre or 'Debt Doctor', that help people systematically get out of the circle of debt.

When a society goes through such sudden transformations to ape foreign markets, it falls into many troubles that stem from a lack of awareness. Let's always remember that at the end of the day, if you live beyond your means on credit cards and personal loans, they will lead you into financial ruin.

The American poet Richard Armour wittily quipped, 'That money talks, I'll not deny. I heard it once. It said "Goodbye".'

Leverage

What, then, is the title of this step speaking of? Can debt ever be good? First things first. Debt is simply borrowing money to spend on things we cannot otherwise afford to buy on our current income streams. But never forget this: debt is expensive because it usually comes with high double-digit interest rates in India. It hampers your savings, it decimates your investing and probably the worst of all, it is highly stressful for your mental makeup.

Is there really something called 'good debt'? Well, let's look at it like this: taking on debt is the easiest way of raising capital. What you choose to do with the capital has the power to make the debt good or bad. It's quite simple:

- Debt for mindless consumption, like buying an expensive gadget you want but don't need: Bad!
- Debt raised for investing in property, business, or something that will generate

long-term income, higher education, for instance: Good!

So while facing any situation that necessitates a loan, we must evaluate whether it is good debt or bad debt. Let's get into the details.

Good debt

- An investment that will grow in value and/or produce long-term returns. Good debt makes you richer.
- Good debt is necessary and sustainable. It's necessary because it can improve your productive capacity. It is sustainable because it enhances your future income, which makes paying it off less of a worry.
- If handled wisely, debt can be used to your advantage. It can help you reach a dream, which may otherwise remain unfulfilled. It can generate manifolds returns in the future. But mark my words: *if* used wisely.

Bad debt

- A liability that takes you farther away from your financial goals. Bad debt makes your poorer.

- Bad debt is debt incurred to purchase things that lose their value immediately after purchase and do not generate long-term income. It means that you're borrowing money to own something whose value starts depreciating from the word go.
- Taking on debt for things you neither need nor can afford is probably the worst crime you can commit against yourself. Think about it, one day at the mall you pass by a fancy clothing store filled with beautiful people. You could be one of them, you think. Sure, your bank balance is running low, and the electricity bill will be soon due, but this is what credit cards are for, right? Wrong!
- Bad debt builds up when you spend more than you can afford. A simple rule of thumb, which served our parents' generation well, if you cannot afford it, live without it.
- It's easy to get stuck in the whirlpool of bad debt. It usually carries the highest interest rate (think credit cards), and it can be unimaginably pricey on delayed payments. For example, credit cards carry interest payments that make the charges grow exponentially. Some credit cards charge an interest rate of over 30%. This means that the outstanding balance doubles in two-and-a-half years!

Let us go through some examples of common types of debt and evaluate whether they are good or bad.

- **Education loan = Good debt.** Usually education loans are an investment in your future. A professional degree gives you a better chance at a brighter future with a higher salary. It increases your value as an employee or entrepreneur. As an added bonus, the interest paid on education loans is tax deductible.
- **Credit card bill that exceeds your bank balance = Bad debt.** Credit card debt is bad because you're not earning any returns on your purchases. The first step towards setting up a solid financial plan for yourself is to get out of credit card debt, if you have any. Never charge your credit card for more than what you can pay each month.
- **A loan to invest in your business = Good debt.** A loan to develop or start your own business is good debt. However, make sure that the loan is realistic and based upon a solid business plan. If done properly, the business gives you a chance at building a sustainable income that will not only help you pay off your loan but further grow the money substantially.
- **Real estate loan = Good debt.** The journalist, Doug Larson, once sarcastically commented,

'People are living longer than ever before, a phenomenon undoubtedly made necessary by the thirty-year mortgage!' Frankly, a real estate loan can be beneficial as it gives you a chance to buy your own home, which gives you stability. If you rent out your home, it becomes an income-generating asset for you. However, do not take on more mortgage than you can comfortably repay. Also, when taking home loans, make sure to read the fine print before signing on the dotted line.

- **Financial loan = Proceed with caution.** Some banks offer loans for buying financial products. Many experienced investors believe that if they can borrow money and make financial investments in stocks or bonds where the return potential is higher than the cost of borrowing, they can pocket the difference and become rich without investing much. My advice: be very careful. Markets are volatile and a dip can create margin calls that can send you in a downward spiral. Many millionaires have become bankrupt on the back of such loans.

How much is too much? A rule of thumb: experts say that no more than 36% of your pre-tax income should go towards servicing debt. This includes your home loan, car loan and credit card bills.

Good debt vs. Bad Debt

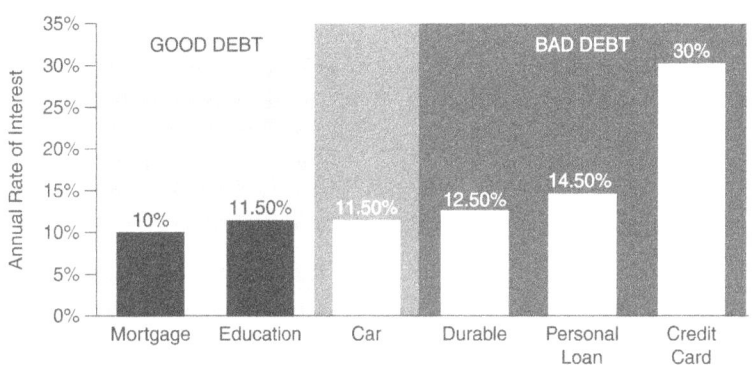

If we look at the table above, it illustrates the various buckets of interest rates charged for different categories of loans. Mortgage (home loans) and education loans are the cheapest, helping you create an asset. Auto loans are a near-necessity in today's times. But while we would all like to own a Mercedes-Benz or a BMW, the right thing to do here is to purchase a vehicle whose loan does not burden you financially. Ultimately, a vehicle is meant for one purpose. To get from Point A to Point B.

If you are borrowing to purchase durables, a holiday or are constantly revolving the dues on your credit card, let me warn you that you are heading for trouble. If you find yourself in this situation, tackle the most expensive loans first. Sometimes, it may even be worth it to take a cheaper personal loan and clear out the dues on your more expensive credit card debt.

Taking good debt is the strategy of using borrowed money to increase return on an investment. If the return on the total value invested in the security (your own cash plus borrowed funds) is higher than the interest you pay on the borrowed funds, you can make significant profit. Use of leverage can be applied to real estate, stocks, bonds, commodities, currencies and other investments but the golden rule is to tread with immense caution.

Debt costs money: Use it wisely

Bad decisions are a part of human nature. We yield to temptation and wild optimism. We give in to sentiments. It's only natural. But sometimes, these decisions can land us in a bad financial situation. So when you're feeling emotional, exercise restraint. Keep in mind that only some forms of debt can be good. Also, sometimes even good debt can turn bad so do your research before incurring it. Be mindful of your payments, interest rates and hidden clauses like repayment penalties and lock-ins. And remember, if someone is trying to sell something to you on the back of a 'Zero Per Cent Loan Scheme', be extra careful. There are no free lunches. The more watchful you will be of debt, the closer you will get to leading the lifestyle you desire.

Key Takeaways

- Debt for mindless consumption, like buying an expensive gadget you want but don't need is bad debt.
- Debt raised for investing in property, business, or something that will generate long-term income, like a higher education is good debt.
- No more than 36% of your pre-tax income should go towards servicing debt.
- Even good debt can turn bad. Be mindful of your payments, interest rates and hidden clauses like repayment penalties and lock-ins.

Step 13

Tax saved is income earned

Let me begin this step with a witty little story: One day at a local restaurant, a lady suddenly shouted, 'My daughter is choking. She accidentally swallowed a five-rupee coin. Is there anyone who can help? Please!' Almost immediately a rather ordinary-looking man who was seated at the nearby table rushed over. He told the mother that he was experienced in handling such situations. He stepped behind the girl, wrapped his arms around her abdomen and squeezed. Out popped the coin! The man returned to his table as if nothing special had happened. 'Thank you,' said the relieved mother. 'Are you a doctor, sir?' she asked. 'No,' replied the man. 'I am an Income Tax Officer.'

It was Benjamin Franklin who famously quipped, 'In this world nothing can be said to be certain, except death and taxes!' And that's precisely the reason why you need to plan your tax liability. Even if you've done everything that we talked about so far...you've saved and invested, created additional income streams and harnessed the power of compounding. And then you find that at the end of the year you have to part with a significant chunk of your earnings to the Income Tax Department. Hurts, no?

Don't get me wrong. I'm not for a moment suggesting that you should evade taxes. I'm simply suggesting that you should use all the legal means at your disposal to reduce your tax liability to the best extent possible.

You may not realize it but taxes are everywhere. Your income is taxed in the form of income tax. Your consumption is also taxed by way of indirect taxes such as service tax, central excise, value added tax, octroi etc. (these are indirect taxes, which are likely to eventually be consolidated into a nationwide GST). For the purpose of this step, however, we will restrict our discussion to direct tax on individuals.

The Indian Income Tax Act allows for several 'deductions' or 'exemptions' that can be claimed by a taxpayer. Exemptions are those parts of your income that do not require to be included in your taxable income calculation. Deductions are those allowances that can be subtracted from your total income thus allowing you to calculate your tax liability on a lower income base as per the rates and slabs in force at that given time. These exemptions and deductions can help you lower your overall tax pay out.

There are obviously limitations to how much in-depth tax knowledge I can impart within one chapter and you will probably have to take specialized advice from a Chartered Accountant or use a filing website such as cleartax.com to plan or file your returns but the intention of this step is to simply give you an overview of the sort of exemptions and deductions that could help you reduce your annual tax burden. Some of the key areas in which you could consider tax savings are:

Life Insurance

Life insurance is considered as a viable tax planning tool because premium paid for life insurance of the taxpayer, spouse or children is treated as tax deductible (up to a certain maximum limit prescribed by the relevant section of the Income Tax Act). The advantage here is that there are multiple life insurance players (including private and public sector companies) and they offer term insurance policies, unit-linked investment policies, pension policies as well as money-back policies.

Public Provident Fund

The Public Provident Fund (or PPF) offers an investment opportunity combined with assured returns combined and income tax benefits. The maturity period is fifteen years and the minimum deposit is Rs 500 per year. Partial withdrawal is allowed during the lock-in period. Currently the interest rate on PPF is 8.10% per year. Again, investments in PPF are treated as tax deductible up to the limit prescribed by the relevant section of the Income Tax Act.

Residential Property

An individual taxpayer can claim a deduction for construction, purchase or expansion of a residential property. If you are paying the principal or interest of a home loan, bearing stamp duty, registration or transfer costs or paying instalments to a cooperative society, all of these can be treated as deductible up to the prescribed maximum. A deduction is also allowed for the interest paid on a loan taken for home repairs although you cannot deduct principal repayments.

Children's Education

To encourage education, the government allows individuals to claim tuition fees paid to any university, college or school in India as deductions within the overall prescribed limit. Other possible deductions include hostel fees and maintenance allowances.

Health Insurance

Health insurance usually covers expenditure incurred towards medical treatment and hospitalization. Health insurance plans in India include hospitalization policies, hospital daily cash benefit plans and critical illness plans. Premium paid is deducted from the total income, again, subject to the maximum limit prescribed.

Shares, securities and deposits

Investment in mutual funds, five-year post office deposits, notified bonds of NABARD, five-year term deposits with scheduled banks, Unit Linked Insurance Plans (ULIP) of the LIC, pension funds of UTI and other MFs, senior citizens' saving schemes, national savings certificates, schemes of the National Housing Bank etc. can also be eligible for deductions up to the prescribed maximum.

Capital gains from residential property

Say you own a house and decide to sell it. The gains arising from the sale are subject to capital gains tax. But if you decide to reinvest the money into a new residential house then the amount that you reinvest could be deducted from your capital gains liability subject to certain conditions.

House Rent Allowance

House Rent Allowance (or HRA) is one of the most common inclusions in the overall pay package of an employee. Individuals can claim exemption of the lowest of (a) rent paid less 10% of salary (b) 50% of basic salary (c) actual HRA received. Of course, this exemption is available only up to a prescribed maximum.

Leave Travel Concession

Your annual holiday also gets you an exemption. The exemption is limited to the economy class fare for the shortest route available to your vacation destination but no exemption is available for hotel, local conveyance etc.

Leave Encashment

If you haven't availed of leave and decide to encash it instead, you are entitled to a lifetime exemption up to Rs 3,00,000. This is only available to you if you are no longer in the employment of the company i.e., upon switching jobs or retirement.

Gratuity

If you switch jobs after having worked with a given company for five years or more or if you retire after 5+ years of service, you will be entitled to a gratuity payment. Up to a maximum amount of Rs 10,00,000 of gratuity is exempt from tax during your lifetime.

Employee Provident Fund

The employer's contribution to PF is taxable if it exceeds a certain maximum per year. The employee's share is eligible for deduction under the overall cap.

Tax-free bonds

Tax-free bonds are similar to other coupon instruments (fixed income securities) that provide a fixed income. However, the interest income from tax-free bonds is exempt from income tax. Redemption of the bonds, however, will attract tax.

Dividends

Dividend that you earn from from shares or units of mutual funds are tax-free up to a maximum of Rs 10 lakh a year.

Long-term Capital Gains on Shares and MFs

Long-term capital gains on sale of listed shares and equity-oriented mutual funds are also exempt from tax. To be eligible for long-term capital gains exemption, these securities need to be held for a period of at least twelve months.

ESOPs

Employee Stock Option Plans (or ESOPs) are frequently offered by companies, particularly start-ups. An ESOP enables an employee to buy shares of the employer company in the future at a discounted price. The tax liability from an ESOP only arises when an employee is actually allotted shares. What this means is that an ESOP is far more tax efficient for an employee than receiving a plain-vanilla salary that instantly attracts tax.

Others

Other areas in which exemptions and deductions can be claimed include (a) amounts paid by you towards medical expenses of elderly parents who can no longer be covered by insurance (b) deductions for those who are differently abled (c) expenditures for preventive health check-ups (d) donations towards social, charitable or philanthropic causes covered under the relevant section.

Please remember that tax planning is as important to wealth creation as savings and investment planning. In recent years, governments around the world have tightened their mechanisms to identify taxable income and bring it into the tax net. You simply need to identify the best provisions within the law that can help you save your hard-earned money.

Key Takeaways

- Tax planning is as important to wealth creation as savings and investment planning.
- Saving taxes can happen by way of exemptions or deductions. It is in your interest to know all the exemptions and deductions that are applicable to you.

Step 14

Learn from those who made it

The title of this book is *13 Steps to Bloody Good Wealth* and you're wondering what a fourteenth chapter is doing in the book. Think of it as the 'no-claim bonus' that you receive on a car insurance policy. The fact that you're here means that you've stayed with me through the thirteen steps. You now deserve a bonus chapter for your persistence!

On a flight to America, I was watching the popular HBO sitcom *Silicon Valley*. In one of the episodes, a wealthy investor is plunged in gloom. He sprawls face-down on a plush sofa inside his sprawling Palo Alto mansion and announces, dramatically, that his life is over. Why? Because his net worth has been reduced to $967,000,000. In other words, he's no longer a billionaire.

It's an ironic scene, meant to make the viewers laugh. The no-longer-a-billionaire chap acts like a broken hero from a Manoj Kumar movie, even though he's still almost a billionaire. But therein lies the difference. 'I'm no longer a part of the three-comma club,' he wails.

The phrase stuck with me. What makes this three-comma club so exclusive? Well, there are only 2325 US dollar billionaires in our world. Let me put this in perspective: for every three million people on earth, there is only one billionaire. Which means that there is one billionaire for the entire population of Oman. On the other hand, can you guess the number of US dollar millionaires in the world? Twelve million.

What makes billionaires so rare? Is there something we can learn from this breed, and apply it to our lives? And who are these elusive people? Let's start with looking at the billionaires of India. India's billionaires are a diverse group, representing a mix of industries, communities, education and cities. First, some numbers:

- The average age of a self-made billionaire is sixty-one. There are only three self-made billionaires under the age of fifty in India and the youngest is forty-one years old.
- The average year when the self-made billionaires incorporated their company is 1980. This means that on an average, it has taken them thirty-five years to reach the billionaire list.

- 26% of India's self-made billionaires have made their fortune in pharmaceuticals, healthcare and related industries.
- 10% of India's self-made billionaires have made their fortune in software and IT services.
- 12% of India's self-made billionaires have made their fortune in real estate.
- 25% of Indian billionaires are Marwaris

Now, let's pick through the facts we have above. First of all, what is the one thing common between all these billionaires? Well, they all are entrepreneurs. In other words, they work for themselves. Make no mistake. A plain vanilla job is unlikely to make you a billionaire even though it could make you very wealthy. Consider this my parting advice after thirteen steps: Success comes to those who're willing to take the risk to follow their passion.

The Parsi Actor who Followed his Passion

The story of this Parsi businessman starts in Mumbai. His father was an executive at a British firm and the boy was sent to Cathedral and John Connon School and Sydenham College for his studies. While the father was keen that the boy develop a 'serious' vocation, the boy was interested in theatre and became enthusiastically involved in acting in plays alongside theatre personalities like Pearl and Alyque Padamsee. But he had to give up his passion in order to start a toothbrush factory!

But the lure of entertainment was too great. In 1981 he set up a cable TV networking company that provided three hours of uninterrupted viewing of films by means of a cable service. The service was limited to the Cuffe Parade area of Mumbai and was made available to the affluent residents of that area at a fee of Rs 200 per month. The service took off and provided the businessman with capital for his next endeavour.

He now turned to making ad films and selling airtime on India's monopoly TV network, Doordarshan. He followed it up by producing TV serials. The ultimate step was production and distribution of movies and TV programs and web content.

In January 2014, he exited the company he founded for a massive premium. His name? Ronnie Screwvala. The company? UTV which was eventually acquired by Disney. Ronnie has been named on Esquire's List of the 75 Most Influential People of the 21st Century and ranked 78 among the 100 most influential people in the world on the Time 100. He was also listed amongst Asia's 25 Most Powerful by Fortune Magazine.

In her book, *The MBA Bubble*, Mariana Zanetti says, 'If you want to be wealthy, at some moment of your life, you will have to create a source of income other than your salary. This is an evident and crushing reality:

If you sell your time to others, you will quickly reach a limit in your capacity to generate income.' Similarly, in his mega successful book, *Rich Dad, Poor Dad*, Robert Kiyosaki insists that the rich do not work for money. Rather, they generate assets that work for them.

My first job right out of college was to sell Windows PCs to stockbrokers. The year was 1991 and desktop computers were the latest fad, albeit one that apparently no one needed. I used to start on the twenty-fifth floor of the Bombay Stock Exchange and work my way down the floors trying to convince dhoti-clad brokers in corridors to buy a computer. I hated the job. I quit within a week and since then, have never worked for anyone but myself and that has brought me far.

Let me illustrate this with a breakdown of how the 400 highest earning people filing income tax returns in America earned their money.

- Wages and salaries: 8.6%
- Interest: 6.6%
- Dividends: 13%
- Partnerships and corporations: 19.9%
- Capital gains: 45.8%
- Others: 6.1%

Those earning wages are less than ten per cent of the top 400 income tax payers. Ninety per cent are those who derive their income from other sources— those related to investments and entrepreneurship.

Keep in mind though that many entrepreneurs may have started out as employees and may have continued to do precisely that for several years before striking out on their own.

Marwari Mantras

You must have noticed above that 25% of India's billionaires are Marwari. This is despite them comprising only 3% of the total Indian population. Doesn't it make you wonder: what are the Marwaris doing differently to consistently reach the billionaire bracket?

Originally from Mewar in Rajasthan, Marwaris travelled to other parts of the country in the 1800s. Most Marwaris rose to fame trading with the East India Company. By 1918 when the First World War ended, they controlled a large part of India's inland trade. Spotting an opportunity, they mastered the process of obtaining industrial licenses and set up one manufacturing unit after another. By the 1970's, they held most of India's private industrial assets.

Of course, the turn of history has a lot to do with one's fortunes. Like many other people, for me, too, it was about being in the right place at the right time. But one has to be aware of the shifting winds and seize the day. In the two decades that followed India's independence, the textiles industry was where the party was. If you've ever strolled through the erstwhile mill complexes in Mumbai's Lower Parel, you will know that those times have long gone. The mills have now been transformed into malls, high-end restaurants, hotels, spas, clubs, boutiques, corporate offices and residential towers.

The seventies and eighties were all about manufacturing. This was pre-liberalisation India, still far away from the allure of globalization and a time when everything was being manufactured in-house. The post-liberalisation years of the nineties and the first decade of the twenty-first century rang with the siren song of financial services, IT services, pharmaceuticals and real estate. And finally today when everyone from high school kids to my neighbourhood *bhajiwalla* are glued to sending and receiving photos using WhatsApp on their smart phones, the agile era of technology and Internet has come upon us.

The trick is to not just spot the trends, but to be able to switch in and switch out smartly. Also, each cycle inevitably brings with it a bevy of fads. You need to be mindful so that you can separate the grain from the chaff. To be honest, some of these calls that you will take are decisions of a lifetime. They surely don't come easy. It's hard work that requires focus and a heavy dose of determination. Mind you, this applies equally to entrepreneurs, investors and professionals.

Going back to India's most successful community, the Marwaris, Thomas A. Timberg was so intrigued by them that he wrote a book called *The Marwaris – From Jagat Seth to the Birlas*. In the book Timberg compares the work ethics of the Marwaris with the West's Protestant ethic of 'thrift, hard work and rationality'. Frankly, these aren't just the rituals of successful Marwaris. They are the rituals of successful people everywhere. According to Timberg, Marwaris are disciplined and still stick to principles such as:

- 'Watch the money.'
- 'Delegate but monitor.'
- 'Plan but have a style and system.'
- 'Lead to expand.'
- 'Do not let the system inhibit growth.'
- 'Do not get blown away by fads.'
- 'Do not miss new developments.'

Timberg also speaks of how flexibility of mind is an important factor in the Marwaris' success. He applauds their adaptability as times change. He credits G. D. Birla's appetite for risk for his colossal success in the jute industry. Keep in mind that combined with risk comes austerity. G. D. Birla famously wrote to his grandson Aditya Birla, then studying at the famous Massachusetts Institute of Technology, 'And above all, don't be extravagant.'

The traits mentioned above are all wise and wonderful habits, not just of Marwaris but of anyone successful. Let me summarise these habits, the final link

in our quest for the common thread that binds all successful people:
- They are not afraid of failure. They like to take calculated risks.
- When they fail, they learn from their mistakes.
- They follow their passions and are competitive.
- They start small but think big.
- They are focused, committed and hard working.
- They believe in themselves.
- They are frugal and don't believe in extravagance.

It's often easier to deride the successful, crediting their success to wealthy forefathers and ancestors but statistically, 60% of billionaires have created their wealth themselves.

Like I mentioned previously in this book, I love the finality of numbers. I take comfort in their unquestionable proof. In this spirit, below are some statistics about India's billionaires that should give you an idea of the who, where and what.

Which industries are thriving?

More than 20% of India's billionaires have made their fortune in the pharmaceutical industry. These pharma kings are benefiting from an industry that's enjoying double-digit growth. McKinsey & Co predicts that

India's pharma market will grow to $55 billion by 2020.
- Pharma, healthcare and related industries — 22 billionaires
- Real estate — 11 billionaires
- Automobiles and parts — 10 billionaires
- Software, IT and related — 9 billionaires
- Financial Services, banking and investments — 7 billionaires
- Oil, gas, petrochemicals, chemicals, mining — 7 billionaires
- Consumer goods — 6 billionaires
- Power — 4 billionaires

Which communities are thriving?

Some communities have performed far better than others in the billionaire rankings. 42% or two in every five billionaires in India is a Marwari or Gujarati.
- Marwari (3% of population) — 25% of billionaires
- Gujarati (4.5% of population) — 17% of billionaires
- Punjabi (2.8% of population) — 13% of billionaires
- Malayali (3.2% of population) — 7% of billionaires
- Sindhi (3% of population) — 6% of billionaires

- Kannada (3.7% of population) — 6% of billionaires
- Tamil (5.9% of population) — 6% of billionaires
- Parsi (0.06% of population) — 4% of billionaires
- Telugu (7.2% of population) — 4% of billionaires
- Bihari (8% of population) — 1% of billionaires

Does education have anything to do with it?

Life is short. The moment you turn fifteen, parents, teachers, relatives, even long lost family friends start murmuring about career and higher education. Things are more relaxed in the West, but in our country, what you study in college is made out to be the key to success. We can spend several hours talking about whether this has some truth or not, but first let's see how Indian billionaires fare when it comes to education.

- Management/business degree — 32% of billionaires
- Engineering — 19% of billionaires
- Science — 16% of billionaires
- Liberal arts — 10% of billionaires
- Medicine — 4% of billionaires
- Pharmacy — 3% of billionaires

- Law — 2% of billionaires
- Others — 6% of billionaires
- No degree/dropout — 8% of billionaires

So, should you become your own boss?

Robert Kiyosaki, the bestselling author of *Rich Dad, Poor Dad* famously said, 'The problem with having a job is that it gets in the way of getting rich.' It is not impossible to become a *crorepati* while working a traditional job. But such wealth comes to a select few, that too after many years of work. When you work for someone as a professional, you get paid a salary, which is then subject to tax. Your salary grows over time, hopefully keeping pace with inflation and giving you hikes based on promotions. But the real fruits of your hard work (the company's profits) belong to its shareholders. Of course, along with the increased returns of running your own business come increased risks.

Keep in mind though that if your company offers some form of employee stock ownership plans as a part of your compensation package, you can also participate in the profits that you are generating.

Interestingly, a Barclays survey of global high net worth individuals showed that entrepreneurship has overtaken inheritance as the main source of wealth creation in the world. What's even more fascinating to know is that high net worth individuals in India are more likely to have made their wealth from a business than their peers in countries such as the US and UK. In fact, 59% of HNIs in India have earned their wealth by building their own business!

This is a very significant number. What's the reason behind this shift? Globalisation, technology and the rise of emerging markets have created an era that is highly suited to individual enterprise. Happily, 84% of the HNIs surveyed said that compared to the past, wealth can be created much faster today. Tap any student in one of India's top B-schools on the shoulder and ask them what they want to be in life. Without batting an eyelid, many of them will say, 'An entrepreneur.' Imagine, then, the kind of earnings you can have access to when you have your own venture.

Let me be clear though. Entrepreneurship is not for everyone. Only you are the best judge of whether you are capable of breaking out on your own. But the pace at which you can create and grow your wealth is far greater when you do.

Wealth and success

In his book *Wealth: An Owner's Manual*, Michael Stolper notes that the three ways to become wealthy are:

- Winning the lottery
- Saving money over a really long period of time and
- Owning your own business.

The chances of someone winning the lottery are so incredibly low (averaging one in a million) that there is no point even discussing the option. Saving and investing money over a really long period of time is wise (and I advise you to do it by following the steps laid out in this book) but the issue lies in the solution itself. It takes a really, really long time, possibly your entire life, to become seriously wealthy.

The Garage Operator Turned Cabbie

Neeraj Gupta's company had its origins in a rundown garage in Oshiwara, Mumbai, among fifty other ragtag garages lining the road. Neeraj started offering Annual Maintenance Contracts (AMCs) to individuals and corporates from this garage in 1998. He called it 'Elite Class'.

His services began to be appreciated by his customers because he offered free breakdown assistance and annual service contract rates that were lower than the competition. In addition was his personalized service. The garage enabled him to build relationships in the corporate sector.

One day he got to know that Tata InfoTech was planning to contract for a bus service for the transportation of their employees. Using the profits of the garage, Neeraj invested Rs 14 lakhs, bought a bus and commenced the shuttle service for Tata. Over the next four years, his company added 1300 vehicles to their fleet, having tied up with multiple corporate entities.

In 2006, Neeraj applied for a taxi service license being offered by the Maharashtra government. Capital was a challenge and India Value Fund, a private equity firm came on board. The first 30 taxis could now go on the road. The company's name? Meru Cabs.

More and more people today are realising that immersing oneself in the creation of a successful business is not only fulfilling but also a way to the kind of wealth which otherwise remains unavailable in a salaried job. You will recall that we spoke of the necessity of creating additional sources of income earlier on in this book. I believe that it can become a stepping stone to eventually being your own boss.

Here's the thing. When you have your own business, not only do you earn income from the profits of the business but you also own the growing value of the enterprise. This beats the 10% annual salary hike by many miles.

Risk and return revisited

As we saw earlier, returns are fully dependent on the risks you are willing to take. In this case, the risks of starting a business are many. First, you will forgo your salary for a year or two, then you will have to dip into your savings or seek capital from friends and family to invest in your dream venture. Mind you, these are just the financial risks. If you get past this phase, you will then have to bear other business uncertainties such as market risks and execution risks. So the potentially high returns associated with an entrepreneurial venture are also accompanied by significantly high risks.

The American economist (and father of value investing) Benjamin Graham has rightly said that 'Every new investment decision bears the risk of being a mistake.'

On the face of it, this book is about wealth. But while writing it, I was convinced that this book is actually about something bigger. Something more meaningful than plain money. Ambition.

The famous English writer D. H. Lawrence said, 'A man is as big as his desire.' Since we live in the equal-opportunity, twenty-first century, I'd like to tweak this to 'A person is as big as his or her desire.' But the key question here is: Desire for what? You are the only one who can define that.

Ambition, like your idea of wealth, your risk appetite and your asset allocation, is a unique beast, individual to you and only you. To define your ambition, ask yourself this: 'What is it that makes me want to get out of bed in the morning?'

The Distributor Who Gave Up Distributing

He was born in the small town of Amreli in Gujarat in 1955. Having completed a B.Com. from the University of Calcutta, he started work as a distributor for generic drugs. It was during this stint that he toyed with the idea of manufacturing his own products rather than simply distributing other companies' goods.

He established a small company with a paid-up capital of Rs 10,000 in 1982 in Vapi, Gujarat. Initially, the company only manufactured five formulations, all in the field of psychiatry. But over the years the product portfolio grew. By 1997 he was ready to acquire a loss-making American company that would give him global reach. He turned around that company very quickly.

Today his pharmaceuticals conglomerate, Sun Pharma, is India's largest drug maker and most valuable drug company. Sun Pharma also ranks fifth in the global generic drugs market. As of 2015, Dilip Shanghvi, the founder, surpassed Mukesh Ambani as the richest person in India.

Money vs. ambition

Narayan Murthy, one of the founders of Infosys, wryly commented, 'Progress is often equal to the difference between mind and mindset.' True. Had Murthy not quit his job at Patni Computer Systems to establish Infosys, the rest of the success story would never have played out.

Frederick Herzberg, a famous psychologist who is remembered for his ground-breaking assertions in business management, held that that the most powerful motivator for people isn't money. Instead, it's the opportunity to learn, grow, contribute, and be recognised. For me, this is what entrepreneurship is about.

American President Franklin D. Roosevelt, quite correctly observed that 'Happiness is not in the mere possession of money; it lies in the joy of achievement, in the thrill of creative effort.' So think about it. What drives you?

When you go to work, are you spending time and energy on only the short-term goals? On the latest presentation that you made? The complicated spreadsheet that you created? These are great distractions that hide the larger goal. Are you propelled forward by a higher, clearer sense of purpose that gives meaning to your daily, repetitive behaviour?

When you focus on only the short-term goals, you can't see the final destination that your path is taking you to. And if you cannot see your endpoint, probably no one else can either. In his book *Brain Drain: The Breakthrough That Will Change Your Life*, Charles F. Glassman says, 'The mistake many of us make is the need and want for short-term gains (immediate gratification), which often leads to long-term pain.'

Are you a manager or a leader?

Now, you may be the best manager your company has ever had. You may be climbing up the ranks faster than anyone else, with salary hikes that make your colleagues turn green with envy. But if you have so much talent, why aren't you focusing those efforts on building your own venture? Dhirubhai Ambani, the founder of Reliance, once said, 'If you don't build your dream, someone else will hire you to help them build theirs.'

Look, a company needs both managers and leaders. But there are some inherent differences between the two. Managers are trained to solve problems, embrace processes and bring stability. On the other hand, leaders are all about innovation and creativity. In fact, some compare entrepreneurs to artists and scientists in their vision to disrupt the existing status quo. Leaders are passionate, inspiring and have a vision that drives success. Imagination and invention are their badge of pride.

John D. Rockefeller III said that in organisations, 'the cards are set up in favour of the proven way of doing things and against the taking of risks.' If you don't want to be a cog in the wheel then you should consider striking out on your own. That decision can be life changing. Most entrepreneurs are inspired by their desire to shake up the system, however difficult it may be.

Only *you* can answer the question about whether you are better as a manager or as a leader or whether you are better as an employee or as an owner.

The Flower That Blossomed

A young man completed his schooling from Bharatiya Vidya Bhavan and Manav Mandir High School and then went to KC College where he earned a B.Sc. He spent a year at IIFT studying the import-export trade and then took up a job at Srinivas Exports, a small export house.

He subsequently gained admission into IIM Ahmedabad where he completed his MBA in Finance. Armed with that MBA, his next stop was ICICI where he began dealing with several export-oriented companies.

One of those clients was Infosys and the young man began thinking about becoming an entrepreneur but was still undecided. He eventually left ICICI to join a small boutique firm called Prime Securities as their head of research and investments.

Eventually the entrepreneurial bug bit him. He quit Prime Securities in 1996 to start up a boutique financial services company along with a colleague from ICICI. The office was 480 square feet in size and the team was just five people. The company began assisting dotcom and BPO companies to raise money while continuing to do advisory work that could bring in steady cash.

There was no looking back. Today Rashesh Shah's company, Edelweiss Financial Services Ltd., has an asset base of Rs 29,000 crores with revenue of Rs 2,416 crore. It has presence in Life Insurance, Housing Finance, Mutual Fund and Retail Financial Markets. It serves its 6.3 lakh customers through 5937 employees based out of 248 offices (including eight international offices).

Indians are risk-averse

You've heard this from me earlier. For years, we in India have been inherently risk-averse. If you have a conversation with any of the thousands of teenagers cramming for their board exams or prepping for university entrance exams, they'll tell you their goal is to find a good job at a 'big' company. Some of them will throw the letters M-B-A out there. Most of the times the kids are simply parroting their parents' desires who have doled out love, support and money to them since they were young for this one objective: a safe job.

Remember the MBA aspirants I was talking about earlier? Most end up accepting the high seven-figure salaries that are offered to them at the end of their degrees because it's easy, safe, even comfortable.

This is the main conundrum of being your own boss. It's essentially a high risk, high return game. If you manage to hook the ball, there are two possibilities: you will hit a six or get caught. The problem is that many people don't even pick up the bat because they fear getting caught.

The middle ground

Now, if you don't have the stomach for the risk of starting your own business, no problem. Today there are numerous options for professionals to become wealthy without sacrificing everything but the kitchen sink. India is a hotbed of entrepreneurial activity and joining an innovative venture can be the gateway to the best of both worlds: salary plus stock options.

Stock options can change your compensation graph completely. I was having a conversation with the head of the mortgage business at one of India's private banks. When I asked him about his asset allocation, his answer was ingenious: 'My equity allocation comprises my stock options, and my salary is my fixed income.' At first, I found this strange but as I thought more about it, I realised it makes total sense!

One caveat here. Like all other investment strategies, this too needs time and hard work. This gentleman has been with the same firm for more than two decades, working his way up the ranks to become a business head. His compensation has included stock options for at least fifteen years. If you apply the logic of the power of compounding for over fifteen years to his stock options, you can see how they are worth a lot of money now. Remember though that all the usual risks apply to stock options too. Someone else I know worked for twenty-five years with a European airline, receiving stock options each year. Just when he was reaching retirement age, the airline went bust and his options became worthless.

The Professor Who Built a Pharma Giant
This story starts in 1968. An associate professor at BITS Pilani dreamt that he could come up with ways to fight infectious diseases. Convinced that his dreams were possible, he left his job and borrowed Rs 5,000 from his wife to establish a small pharmaceuticals firm that he named after a flower.

Today, his company, Lupin, is a transnational pharmaceutical company based in Mumbai. It is the seventh-largest company by market capitalization and the tenth-largest generic pharmaceutical company by revenue globally. The professor who started the company, Desh Bandhu Gupta is a billionaire with assets of around Rs 45,000 crores.

No pain, no gain

In my experience, to be a successful entrepreneur you need a thick skin and a nimble mind. Entrepreneurial skills are a mix of guts and wisdom. And here's the truth: you have to give your venture your time, energy and life. Steel yourself for the moment when you see your Facebook feed filled with the photos of your friends' last vacation because while they're sipping cocktails in tropical isles, you will be chipping away at building your dream.

Another piece of advice I give to budding entrepreneurs is to be ready to fail. Resilience has to be in your blood. If you look deeper, you will find that many rockstar entrepreneurs tasted success after many failed ventures. To be a successful entrepreneur, not only do you have to be flexible, inspiring and optimistic, but you also have to treat every flop as a learning gig.

Entrepreneurship is about taking the risk on the back of the idea you believe in. It entails risking your job security, regular salary and social status in order to pursue your idea. The good news? You may succeed and there will be no joy greater than success. And if you're lucky, wealth will automatically come with success.

The Rikshaw Puller Who Pulled in Millions

Mahashay Dharampal Gulati was born in 1923 in Sialkot. After the partition of India in 1947 he arrived in Delhi with Rs 1500 in his pocket. Out of this, he spent Rs 750 to buy a rickshaw. He would ferry passengers each day from New Delhi Railway Station to Qutub Road and from Karol Bagh to Bara Hindu Rao at two annas per passenger.

Fed up of the gruelling schedule, he bought a small 14 feet x 9 feet shop at Ajmal Khan Road in Karol Bagh, New Delhi. He began grinding and selling spices from this shop. Today, the company that he founded is a leading Indian manufacturer, distributor and exporter of ground spices and spice mixtures under the brand name MDH. The company is worth over Rs 500 crores.

Create your own luck

I said 'if you're lucky' above but if you thought I was talking about some crazy idea of being born with providence, sorry, I don't believe in all that. I am convinced that all of us have the power to create our own luck. Our attitude and approach help us increase the number of opportunities that come our way. These are some lucky charms I have picked up in my life, which are succinctly put together in Ashwin Sanghi's book, *13 Steps to Bloody Good Luck*. If you haven't already read this book, I suggest you do it immediately because good luck and good wealth go hand in hand.

- **Build your network:** People like helping each other out. And you never know who you will meet. Remember Li KaShing's expenditure model allocating 20% on building your network?
- **Try new things:** It opens your mind to ideas. It opens you up to opportunities you may not have otherwise thought of.

- **Calculated risks are important:** Risk and return go hand in hand and nowhere is this more valid than for entrepreneurs. But hey, don't take blind risks. Jumping off an airplane without a parachute will take you only one place: down. Don't disregard gravity. Be smart about the risks you take.
- **Learn from mistakes:** In the event of failure, we would all like to retreat into a dark corner to lick our wounds. While that is comforting, what is even better is to evaluate what went wrong and ensure not to make the same mistakes again.
- **Make the best of bad situations.** Remember that you never stop learning.
- **Be alert:** Lucky people are always watchful for opportunities around them.

The path to wealth and success is crooked. During this journey, if you can position your passion and get paid for it, my friend, you have hit true jackpot. Oprah Winfrey, the fabulously wealthy media personality has correctly observed, 'If you do work that you love and the work fulfils you, the rest will come.'

If you really think about it, there is no mystery to becoming wealthy. All the steps that I have outlined for you in this book can be represented in the common sense flowchart below. Master this, and you will have mastered wealth.

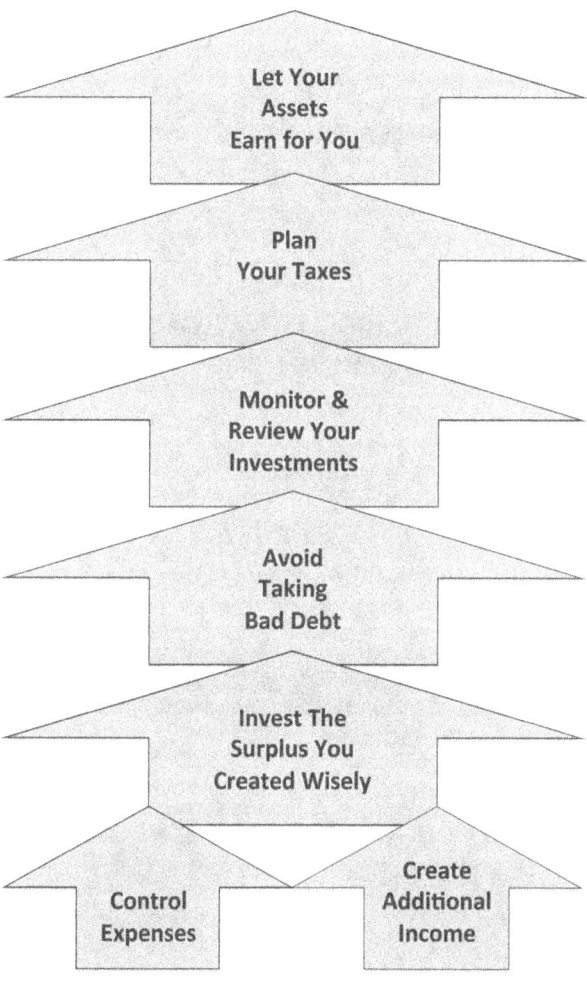

References & Resources

Some of the source material that we utilized while penning this book are mentioned here so that you may further explore the subject.

Books

- *Rich Dad Poor Dad: What the Rich Teach their Kids About Money that the Poor and Middle Class Do Not*, Robert T. Kiyosaki, Perseus Books Group
- *The MBA Bubble: Why Getting an MBA Degree Is a Bad Idea*, Mariana Zanetti, CreateSpace Independent Publishing Platform
- *The Intelligent Investor*, Benjamin Graham, Harper Business
- *Think & Grow Rich*, Napoleon Hill, Amazing Reads
- *Freakonomics: A Rogue Economist Explores the Hidden Side of Everything*, Steven D. Levitt, William Morrow

- *Day to Day Economics*, Satish Y. Deodhar, Random House India
- *The Tipping Point: How Little Things Can Make a Big Difference*, Malcolm Gladwell, Little Brown Book Group
- *The Warren Buffett Way: Investment Strategies of the World's Greatest Investor*, Robert G. Hagstrom, Wiley

Subscription Services

(not recommended for beginners, may lead to information overload)

- ET Wealth (publication)
- Morningstar.com (publication)
- Alphaideas (blog)
- State of the Market (blog)
- subramoney.com (blog)

Online Resources (Free tools)

- Google finance
- Yahoo finance
- Moneycontrol
- ET portfolio
- Perfios
- Aditya Birla My Universe

- Valueresearchonline.com
- Financial planning calculators on insurance company websites
- Mortgage calculators on Housing Finance companies websites
- Tax calculations: Cleartax.com
- Investment/finance definitions and terms: Investopedia.com

Paid Tools for financial planning & execution

- AssetVantage
- Arthayantra
- Mymoneyfrog
- Bigdecisions.in

Online discount brokers/MF transaction engines

- zerodha.com
- rksv.com
- fundsindia.com
- 5nance.com
- All Mutual Fund sites offer investment capabilities online—allow you to invest in direct plans without any fees

Acknowledgements

Many thanks are in order to the wonderful people who made *13 Steps to Bloody Good Wealth* possible.

I'm grateful to my dear friend Ashwin Sanghi for offering me the opportunity to write this book when there were hundreds of other investment advisors who were more qualified than me. My heartiest thank you.

In my journey of researching and writing this book, I was ably helped by my colleagues in the UniDEL group. Deep Chatterjee and Sukriti Mimani found, sifted and analysed vast amounts of information on the subject of wealth. Deep was by my side as I wrote the manuscript, watching over all the numbers.

My editor, Aurvi Sharma and graphic designer, Rachita Dalal, both of Studio 577, helped me craft the message to make it more interesting and engaging.

Thanks are also due to the team at Westland, including Gautam Padmanabhan, Krishna Kumar, Satish Sundaram, Sudha Sadanand, Preeti Kumar, Deepthi Talwar, Jayanthi Ramesh, Vipin Vijay,

Sanyog Dalvi, Gururaj, Sarita Prasad, Naveen Mishra, Shatrughan Pandey and Neha Khanna.

Haitenlo Semy who provided the wonderful cover for this book deserves my gratitude as does Karthik Venkatesh who carried out the editing of this book.

I would also like to thank my father Kishore Dalal for always giving me the freedom to make my own decisions and commit my own mistakes. I wouldn't be who I am without the wisdom I acquired from those experiences.

Last, but certainly not the least, thank you, Mamta, my dear wife, for patiently watching me take on yet another project!

AssetVantage

Let me take you to back to the beginning in order to end this tale.

In the 1920's, my grandfather established a successful brokerage firm in Bombay, Rasiklal Maneklal & Co. In due time, my father diversified into technology ventures and by the 70's we had a solid presence as an engineering and technology firm. So I had the benefit of growing up in a finance and technology environment, which shaped my thinking at an early age.

I got involved with the family-owned business in the early 90's when it was struggling to adapt to the new economic reality of India. We were able to reinvent ourselves and by 2005, we had set up UniDEL Group, a successful venture incubator that takes pride in disruptive innovation by leveraging technology to solve complex problems. We have built several profitable ventures from the ground up leveraging deep operational knowhow and strategic investment.

All this while, we also invested in traditional asset classes including public equities, fixed income and real estate. To manage this properly, I set up a professionally managed family investment office in 2005 with ten people working day in and out to create a monthly MIS (Management Information System) for over forty investing entities. At this time, we were in desperate need of clear, straightforward information for our decision-making. But we kept bumping against information arbitrage. It was difficult to quickly analyse various financial metrics and marry that with the advice that was being dished out to us by leading investment advisors. We tried multiple combinations of existing tracking technology: Tally for books of accounts, Excel for reporting and performance calculations, Money Control for stock and fund prices, and what not.

What we found was that while the free or low-priced tools are not comprehensive enough and therefore unsuitable for most portfolios, the paid ones are too expensive and often linked to a percentage of the size of your investment portfolio (don't ask me why a software company would need know how much money you have!) Many times, a lot of the financial information rested with individual people in our office. And if they left, we were left in a complete lurch.

The real test came in 2008. All hell broke loose during the financial crisis. We tried hard to put temporary bandages and carry out damage control by getting rid of bad investments, but our portfolio had so many close-ended schemes, large exit fees and illiquid asset classes that we could not pull out of all the duds. To my surprise, I had no idea how I had ended up in such a situation. Perhaps it happened because of my inadvertent desire to earn high returns without fully considering all the risks and the fine print.

The need for making quick and good decisions was paramount at this time, and I was frustrated by the lack of clear information about our investments. It's easy to let go of your portfolio while riding the wave during a good phase. But these tough times imprinted upon me the importance of tracking and control.

Given that we were an engineering and technology group, I was shocked at the lack of a comprehensive solution to such a huge, pressing problem. This was a gaping hole that needed to be addressed. So we decided to create our own software platform to manage an all-inclusive book of liquid and illiquid assets combined with a few other important features like accounting. Asset Vantage was born as our twelfth venture at UniDEL.

I firmly believe that to succeed in the coming decades, we need sophisticated yet simple to use technology to manage wealth. Technology should complement our investment strategy, not be a hindrance to it in the form of information overload. This is the problem we decided to solve with Asset Vantage (www.assetvantage.com).

Whichever software platform you choose to use to manage your investments, here is a handy checklist of features that that you should look for:

- **Data aggregation:** Does the software easily aggregate data across all liquid and illiquid asset classes?
- **Accounting:** Can you automatically maintain your books of accounts and information flow with your accounting firm to easily calculate taxes and file returns on time?
- **Analytics:** Can you quickly see what investments and advisors are performing as promised and if you are taking any undue risks or losing any great investment opportunities?
- **Back-office:** Can you easily manage your paper records, create alerts and reminders and generally be well organized?
- **Security:** Does the software platform allow you to own the data and leave the software at any time by easily exporting all your data out? Is your data secure and are there are hidden issues that you should watch out for?

I wish you well in your journey towards Bloody Good Wealth.

STAY IN CONTROL OF YOUR FINANCIAL LIFE.

Asset Vantage is an intuitive technology platform to help bring your entire financial life in one place.

INVESTMENT ANALYTICS • INTEGRATED ACCOUNTING
DOCUMENT VAULT • WEB & MOBILE APP

Sign up for the AV Personal Edition for free today.

www.assetvantage.com/13steps

Asset Vantage is not a wealth advisor or wealth manager.

www.ingramcontent.com/pod-product-compliance
Lightning Source LLC
LaVergne TN
LVHW010319070526
838199LV00065B/5607